Old Hexhamshire

Compiled by

Hilary Kristensen

Old Hexhamshire

by Hilary Kristensen

First Published November 2014
by Wagtail Press,
Gairshield,
Steel,
Hexham,
Northumberland
NE47 0HS
www.wagtailpress.co.uk
wagtailpress@yahoo.co.uk

Designed by T. W. Kristensen

ISBN 978-0-9559395-3-2

19th century cover paintings:
Front - Dukesfield Corn Mill
Back - The Steel

Wagtail Press
www.wagtailpress.co.uk

Foreword

'Old Hexhamshire' is the second book by Wagtail Press about this
fascinating area; the first book 'Memories of Hexhamshire' was published
15 years ago. Many more photographs have been collected and new
information has been discovered since 1999.
The Hexhamshire Show was held as part of the Millennium celebrations;
this was a great success and a perfect way of reliving an important part
of our local history.
We have a lot to appreciate and remembering our legacy is an important
part of living in Hexhamshire; a beautiful corner of Northumberland.

Thank you to everyone who has kindly contributed towards this book;
especially three ladies who have been particularly helpful and generous:
Nancy Graham, nee Lowdon; Betty Martin, nee White, and Marie
Simpson, nee White.
My sincere thanks also go to Yvonne Purdy and Liz Sobell who have
helped in so many ways.

I would like to dedicate 'Old Hexhamshire' to all the families who have
lived and worked in the 'Shire' over past centuries.

Hilary Kristensen
November 2014

19th century painting of Dye House

The Steel, c.1900

Contents

Page
6   St. Helen's Church
30   Charity Begins at Home
42   School Days
58   The Halliwell Picnic
70   Songs, Stories & Poems
79   In Grateful Memory
82   In Living Memory
90   Blackhall
95   High Holmes
98   The Linnels
106   Newbiggin
112   Riddlehamhope
125   Stotsfold Hall
132   Horse Power
138   Harvest in the 'Shire
142   Shire Families
149   Acknowledgements
150   Index

plate 1

St. Helen's Church 1890

St. Helen's Church

Medieval Period

Whitley Chapel probably originated as a pre-Reformation chapel on a medieval site. The medieval window at the east end appears to have been incorporated into subsequent buildings.

Reverend George Ritschell (1657-1717), Lecturer of Hexham, gave an account of the origins of Whitley St. Helen's in his description of charitable donations in Tynedale. Rev. Ritschell bequeathed 40 shillings per annum to the Minister of Whitley Chapel, and failing a minister there, to the Mercers' Lecturer at Hexham for the poor of Hexhamshire and Slaley Parish.

'There had been in old time a little chapel, by the highway side which leads from the head of the shire to Hexham, where a branch of it turns off to the east to the Steel and Duke's-field mills, dedicated to St. Helen, commonly called Whitley chapel, which had been entirely ruined, and was rebuilt by subscriptions sometime before the restoration, [c.1660] to teach school and the neighbourhood to meet in upon occasion and is set forth in the preamble to remembered.'
To the repairing of the chapel Sir Edward Radcliffe gave three trees, and Sir John Fenwick six trees, out of certain timber in Dotland; and George Bacon of Broadwood-hall, in Allendale, gave a wain load of squared timber out of the wood at Steel-hall.' [1]

1650
The chapel building was being used as a school. *'There is in Hexham Shire A certain Chapple Calld Whitley Chapple wch had been totally ruined but a small thing was erected there to teach a petty school in.'*

1694
'the Quakers from distant parts meeting at the said Chapel hill, and great numbers out of curiosity resorting to them, the said chapel was made fit and appropriated to divine service but … being very mean and not sufficient to contain half the people who resorted thither.'
The curate of Slealy at present preaches there every 14 night, but ye people are so very poor, that their contributions raise little above £9 per annum thoa that part of this Shire be above 9 Northern Miles in length & there were above 700 Souls on that side. [2]

1710
'I must here remark that Whitley Chapel wd [not] have been fit for divine service in bad weather without the sd repairs, that there be some places in the roofe wch ought to be mended this summer, to put of till they can be rebuilt, to preserve the timbar & prevent future damage. This Countrey is very poor at present by reason of the gt decay of the lead trade & want of pay, so that the Church sesse is not yet Collected in the Shire, nor will be till Duxfield pay.' [3]

1715
A survey refers to Whitley Chapel as a 'chapel of ease' dedicated to St. Helen.

1743
Whitley Chapel was now also known as St Helen's Chapel. Entirely taken down and rebuilt when it was again much enlarged: *'a Subscription was again set on foot for Rebuilding this Chapel, and making it Commodious for that part of Hexhamshire.'*
The font, gallery and box pews were installed around this time. Archdeacon Sharp reported to the Archbishop that *'Mr Calverley Blackett gave a bell to this chapel, but the inhabitants have not as yet hung it up for use.'*

1748
'Mr Brown, the present Schoolmaster of Hexham, does duty there every Sunday, for a very small Salary, raised by Subscription, as an Additionall Provision to the 40 Shillgs. P.Ann: left by Mr Ritchell.' [4]

1752
The churchyard ground was established, and rented to churchwardens William Dixon, William Armstrong, Joseph Dodd and George Bell for 1d a year.

1764
The churchyard was consecrated by Robert Drummond, the Lord Archbishop of York, on July 6th.

The estate of Mollersteads was purchased to provide a permanent endowment for a curate. Rev. Abraham Brown, Master at Hexham Grammar School, was appointed as the first perpetual minister for Whitley Chapel. Abraham Brown's beautifully written registers for baptisms, marriages and burials began in July of 1764.

1823

'The congregation in the parish church is comparatively small, which may be accounted for from the state of the seats and the extreme cold. The church is generally more numerously attended in the afternoon than in the morning, the lecture being the attraction'. [5]

1836

Extensive alterations and repairs were undertaken including re-roofing with slates instead of stone and the repair of pews. The church was unfit for services for a long period, partly due to delays caused by the financial problems of rebuilding but also because no curate was in attendance. Christenings and marriages were performed at Slaley or Hexham in the interim period.

1837

The ecclesiastical connection with York was terminated and the church became subject to the See of Durham.

1842

The church was included in the rural deanery of Hexham as part of the archdeaconry of Northumberland and subsequently transferred from the Bishopric of Durham to that of Newcastle.

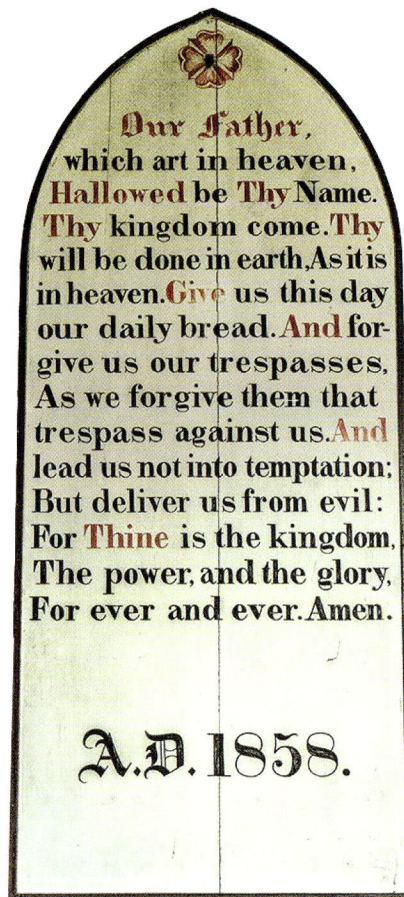

plate 2

The Pater Board

1855

New stoves were installed. A harmonium was purchased c.1868.

1858

Pater board and the Creed and Commandment boards were erected.

1878

May 23rd joiner Richard Tweddle, from Raw Green, made 'one New Box [pew?] for chapel' costing £2 - 4s. and on March 25th 1881 he spent '4 & half days Painting Chapel' at £18 with 4lb white lead at £1 - 8s.

1888

Improvements and repairs were undertaken - *'Repairs to the Building, proper Heating Apparatus, and the beautifying and improvement of the Churchyard'.*

1910

The Bishop of Newcastle re-opened St. Helen's Church on November 25th after restoration. The high pulpit, gallery and box pews had been removed and a new vestry built.

'The place has been re-roofed and the old ceiling replaced with a cleaded and panelled ceiling. The windows on the south and west end have been replaced and lead glazing has been fixed. The gallery is now removed, and the seats extended to the western end of the building. There is now more room for the chancel and communion table at the eastern end. This portion looks very effective, with its Frosterly and Sicilian marble steps and mosaic, as well as new oak communion kneelers.'

Hexham Courant   November 25th 1910

The medieval window at the east end of the church

plate 3

THE LAMENTATIONS OF WHITLEY CHAPEL 1836

Ah! what will come next, can any one say, now?
I'm griev'd and perplext, from day unto day, now,
Such cutting and carving, as they have upon me,
As I'm not deserving, they've nearly undone me;
Nay, I cannot tell, what mean the queer elves,
'Twill be very well, if they know that themselves.

Jacob first took in hand, to slice me one day, now,
The Priest gave command, and he did obey, now,
He set Matt to work, and faith he's a topper,
He wrought like a turk, yet, did as was proper;
Had he stay'd, I believe, 't had been better for me, But
sadly I grieve, for he's gone, do ye see?

Matt pull'd off each lock, when lo! I declare,
He found that my block, was worse than my hair;
My grey pate had brav'd, the storms deadly blast,
As I wish to be sav'd, the dire storms now past;
My skull …. so musht, it might have come down;
In a deluge of dust, and mauld many a crown.

Now Matt cut his stick, he thought it high time,
Of the job he was sick, and where was the crime?
Tho' he could have mended me, he wouldn't stay;
Let no-one offended be, now he's away;
Let no neighbour or brother, his views wrongly scan,
Or, say any other, than "he's a brave man."

When Matt went away, nor longer would tarry,
Who enter'd one day, but good joiner Harry,
Jacob sent him to finish, what Matt had begun,
My fears might diminish, if they were but done
Nay each passer by, now ventures to praise me;
They say, up on high, they purpose to raise me.

Now they've ta'en all the grey, from the top of my pate,
New brain pan they lay, and put on blue slate;
Tho' the grey and I sorted, quite loving together,
And true, as reported, fear'd no kind of weather,
But old friends as we were, it seems we must part,
'Tis enough I declare, to break my poor heart.

Tho' my top well they've done, I'll tell you some news,
They have made pretty fun, in mending my pews;
I'm like an old garment, with patch upon patch,
They've clos'd many a rent, with wood scarcely match;
If quiet I keep, they'll pull me to pieces,
As thorns do the sheep, when they tatter their fleeces.

I was griev'd and thought shame, when some folk came
to church,
Well knowing their aim, they were left in the lurch;
The parson away, 'tis no wonder the sheep,
Should all go-astray, if the shepherd's asleep;
Or what is as bad, if the shepherd's from home,
The case must be sad, if the wolf, then should come.

Some for sacrament come, now sad was their plight,
No Parson at home, they got not the rite;
Some their little ones bring, to christnings, you see,
It was the same thing, the Priest, where was he?
"Off seeing his father, quite out of his parish,"
The people now rather, did feel themselves queerish.

I really am glad, it ne'er enter'd the head
Of a lass or a lad, to come hither to wed;
Had they come at that time, they had not got wedded,
If so, without crime, they could not be bedded,
This need not perplex 'em, at all, I declare,
There's Slaley or Hexham, they'll wed them all there.

Then I lost christening dues, for to Slaley they went;
If thus they me use, I can only lament;
We have a church warden, to give him his due,
He's surely a hard un, nay, but we have two;
And two unto them – one lives on Dick's land,
To the Parson, Ah hem! I see them all cap in hand.

They'll their caps move to him, but not unto me,
Or me they look grim, as grim well can be;
They think me a fash, now, as God is my judge,
To lay out the cash, now, they sadly begrudge;
They should flag well my floor, lest the shrews and the
moles,
Enter "not by the door," but up through the holes.

What my old frame looks like, with blue slates upon it,
I'll tell you by crike, it looks like a donnet;
Tho' the Parson may show't, to master and scholars,
'Tis like Joseph's coat, of various queer colours;
Or a kaleidoscope, or a magpie, nay, worse,
The truth must be spoke, an old piebalded horse.

Ere this patching work ends, it is very plain,
That none of my friends will know me again;
When the lads and the lasses, to me shall repair,
And old folk with glasses, Ah me!, how they'll stare;
On me they may gaze, but I have a notion,
Their too great amaze, may spoil their devotion.

Hexham Church has but been, a cold friend unto me,
She acts like a queen, I mean a queen bee;
She's drained the honey, all out of my hive,
And got all the money, which makes her so thrive;
She dol'd back twenty pounds, then told me, poor elf,
'Twas her charity's bounds….to shift for myself.

Did not Elsdon supply me, and keep up my head,
Who then would come nigh me? nay, I have a dread,
Should this prop, too, give way, unhappy, then I,
On that sad, fatal day, might stand here and cry;
I should then be deserted, my slates and my walls,
Should for ever be parted, and Whitley Church falls.

When this patching shall end, 'twill be a disgrace,
To see your old friend, with quite a new face:
But her heart still is good, tho' crazy each joint,
And 'tis understood, that is the main point;
She still will receive you, 'tho not flagg'd or pav'd,
Come in and "believe now, and you shall be sav'd."

Good people stand by me, and lend me your aid,
They mean still to try me, I'm greatly afraid;
See here a piece old, and there a piece new,
If they had me sold, and got what was due;
A tale I can tell, and it is a true one,
I think they as well, might build me a new one.

May 9th 1836 by M. Wilson, Hexham

THE LAMENTATIONS OF

WHITLEY CHAPEL,

In Hexhamshire, in 1836.

By M Wilson, Hexham.

Ah! what will come next, can any one say, now?
I'm griev'd and perplext, from day unto day, now,
Such cutting and carving, as they have upon me,
As I'm not deserving, they've nearly undone me;
Nay, I cannot tell, what mean the queer elves,
'Twill be very well, if they know that themselves.

Jacob first took in hand, to slice me one day, now,
The Priest gave command, and he did obey, now,
He set Matt to work, and faith he's a topper,
He wrought like a turk, yet, did as was proper;
Had he stay'd, I believe, 't had been better for me,
But sadly I grieve, for he's gone, do ye see?

Matt pull'd off each lock, when lo! I declare,
He found that my block, was worse than my hair;
My grey pate had brav'd, the storms deadly blast,
As I wish to be sav'd, the dire storms now past;
My skull had so musht, it might have come down,
In a deluge of dust, and mauld many a crown.

Now Matt cut his stick, he thought it high time,
Of the job he was sick, and where was the crime?
Tho' he could have mended me, he wouldn't stay;
Let no one offended be, now he's away;
Let no neighbour or brother, his views wrongly scan,
Or, say any other, than "he's a brave man."

When Matt went away, nor longer would tarry,
Who enter'd one day, but good joiner Harry,
Jacob sent him to finish, what Matt had begun,
My fears might diminish, if they were but done
Nay each passer by, now ventures to praise me,;
They say, up on high, they purpose to raise me.

Now they've ta'en all the grey, from the top of my pate,
New brain pan they lay, and put on blue slate;
Tho' the grey and I sorted, quite loving together,
And true, as reported, fear'd no kind of weather,
But old friends as we were, it seems we must part,
'Tis enough I declare, to break my poor heart.

Tho' my top well they've done, I'll tell you some news,
They have made pretty fun, in mending my paws;
I'm like an old garment, with patch upon patch,
They've clos'd many a rent, with wood scarcely match;
If quiet I keep, they'll pull me to pieces,
As thorns do the sheep, when they tatter their fleeces.

I was griev'd and thought shame, when some folk came
to church,
Well knowing their aim, they were left in the lurch;
The parson away, 'tis no wonder the sheep,
Should all go astray, if the shepherd's asleep;
Or what is as bad, if the shepherd's from home,
The case must be sad, if the wolf, then should come.

Some for sacrament come, now sad was their plight,
No Parson at home, they got not the rite;
Some their little ones bring, to christnings, you see,
It was the same thing, the Priest, where was he?
"Off seeing his father, quite out of his parish,"
The people now rather, did feel themselves queerish.

I really am glad, it ne'er enter'd the head,
Of a lass or a lad, to come hither to wed;
Had they come at that time, they had not got wedded,
If so, without crime, they could not be bedded,
This need not perplex 'em, at all, I declare,
There's Slaley or Hexham, they'll wed them all there.

Then I lost christening dues, for to Slaley they went,
If thus they me use, I can only lament;
We have a church warden, to give him his due,
He's surely a hard un, nay, but we have two;
And two unto them—one lives on *Dick's* land,
To the Parson, Ah hem! see them all cap in hand.

They'll their caps move to him, but not unto me,
Or me they look grim, as grim well can be;
They think me a fash, now, as God is my judge,
To lay out the cash, now, they sadly begrudge;
They should flag well my floor, lest the shrews and the
moles,
Enter " *not by the door,*" but up through the holes.

What my old frame looks like, with blue slates upon it,
I'll tell you by crike, it looks like a donnet;
Tho' the Parson may show't, to master and scholars,
'Tis like Joseph's coat, of various queer colours;
Or a kaleidscope, or a magpie, nay worse,
The truth must be spoke, an old piebalded horse.

Ere this patching work ends, it is very plain,
That none of my friends will know me again;
When the lads and the lasses, to me shall repair,
And old folk with glasses, Ah me! how they'll stare;
On me they may gaze, but I have a notion,
Their too great amaze, may spoil their devotion.

Hexham Church has but been, a cold friend unto me,
She acts like a queen, I mean a queen bee;
She's drained the honey, all out of my hive,
And got all the money, which makes her so thrive;
She dol'd back twenty pounds, then told me, poor elf,
'Twas her charity's bounds---to shift for myself.

Did not Elsdon supply me, and keep up my head,
Who then would come nigh me? nay, I have a dread,
Should this prop, too, give way, unhappy, then I,
On that sad, fatal day, might stand here and cry;
I should then be deserted, my slates and my walls,
Should for ever be parted, and Whitley Church falls.

When this patching shall end, 'twill be a disgrace,
To see your old friend, with quite a new face:
But her heart still is good, tho' crazy each joint,
And 'tis understood, that is the main point;
She still will receive you, tho' not flagg'd or pav'd,
Come in and " believe now, and you shall be sav'd."

Good people stand by me, and lend me your aid,
They mean still to try me, I'm greatly afraid;
See here a piece old, and there a piece new,
If they had me sold, and got what was due;
A tale I can tell, and it is a true one,
I think they as well, *might build me a new one.*

May 9th, 1836.

Hexham: *Printed for, and Sold by the Author.*

plate 4

Left- St. Helen's Church as it looked after the extensions and repairs were completed in 1836.

Below - Accounts of income and costs incurred.

1836
Money received towds. Repairs of Whitley

	£	s	d
Greenwich Hospital	21	"	"
Donation from Hexham Church	20	"	"
John Hewitson	10	"	"
Miss Plummer	10	"	"
Messrs Airey & Lee each £5	10	"	"
Sir Thos. Clavering & J.L. Clavering Esqr	10	"	"
Messrs. Ruddock each £5	10	"	"
Revd. J. D. Waddilove	5	"	"
Leonard Wilson Esq.	2	"	"
Mr Pigg, Haydon Bridge	2	"	"
Mr Crawhall Esq.	1	"	"
Mr Johnston Esq. N. Castle	2	"	"
Mrs Errington, Lipwood Well	1	"	"
A. Stokoe Esq. Acomb	1	"	"
John Kirsopp Esq. Hexham	1	"	"
Thos. Adamson Esq.	1	"	"
Sums below one pound	10	4	10
	£117	4	10

Money paid towd. the Repairs of Whitley Chapel

	£	s	d
Jacob Bulman per Contract	84	12	6
Leading Slates – Wood – Lathes &c.	10	9	4
Boarding Pews & Wood for same	4	6	2
Painting &c.	7	7	0
To Robert Graham	1	19	6
Mending Altar Cloth	"	2	6
New Communion Cloths	"	4	2
Wilson's Bill for repairing Windows	"	12	6
Letters & Stamps	"	7	6
Labouring for Chapel		11	6
Travelling Expences &c.	1	16	0
	£112	8	8
Money paid John Robinson for Work &c.	2	11	5
	£115	"	1

	£	s	d
Brought forwd.	117	4	10
Deduct	115	"	1
Money in hand	£ 2	4	9

H. Nanney

STAINED GLASS MEMORIAL WINDOW

A beautiful stained glass window has just been placed in Whitley Church, Hexhamshire, as a memorial to the late Mr. Wm. Angus. The subjects illustrated include the Angel at the Tomb and Christ appearing to Magdalene. It is a most effective window, the colouring being chaste and harmonious, the grouping of the figures being excellent and the expression on the faces very beautiful. At the base of the window the dedicatory inscription runs: -

"To the Glory of God and in memory of William Angus, this window was dedicated by his widow, Isabella Angus."

Owing to indisposition Mrs Angus is confined to her home, and she has asked Mr. Wm. Fisher to unveil the window on her behalf. This ceremony will be performed on Sunday morning.

The late Mr. Wm. Angus was the only son of Mr. Wm. Angus of Low Raw Green and came of an old Hexhamshire family who had farmed at Dye House, Dotland Park, and Low Raw Green for a period extending over 300 years. After farming Low Raw Green for some years, the late Mr. Angus went to Salmons Field, where he remained for 14 years. He was a splendid type of farmer, and was highly esteemed.

Hexham Courant   December 6th 1913

William Angus died August 14th 1896, aged 62;
Isabella died December 20th 1913, aged 70.

plate 5

13

BOX PEWS

Box pews were first installed in churches in the late 17th century but in the case of Whitley Chapel they were probably fitted around 1743 when the church was completely rebuilt.

A box pew consisted of a bench contained within wooden panelled partitions with a hinged door. These were usually owned and maintained by the better off members of the congregation and would often be comfortably fitted out with cushioned seats and mats on the floor. The poorer members of the church used the free seats at the back or had to stand.

By the time the church had been restored and altered in 1910 the gallery had been removed which gave more room for the pews we see today.

When John Lowes of Finechambers Mill wrote his will in 1825, he considered the question of family pews of significant importance:

'And as to the half of the pew in Slaley Church I give and devise the same unto my Son Michael Lowes his Heirs and assigns for ever And as to my Third part of a pew in the Methodist Chapel or Meeting House at Ordley [Finechambers] I give and devise the same unto my son John Lowes his Heirs and Assigns for ever.'

The Honble
Thomas Ricd. Beaumont Esqr.

*The cause of My Address is on account of a Pew or stall
In the Chappel of Hexham-shire*

Viz Henry Dixon My Grandfather who had different Estates in Hexham-shire which he bequeathed to three Daughters, two of which Daughters Married and the Estates left to them was sold by their Husbands and Children and there is none of the Family has any property <u>now</u> in Hexham-shire, but my self who has that portion of Lands & Ground which was left to my Mother. The people who bought different Estates of Robert Dickeson And also of Henry White, never made any Claim to the Pew in the Chappel in Hexham-shire, Until your Hon^r^ *bought a part of the Estate known by the Name of the Stapples. To My great surprise The late Mr Isaac Hunter took possession of the Pew And placed his favourites to sit in it, which deprives me, and my Tennants from sitting there. Hon*^d^ *<u>Sir</u> I hope you will not Claim that Pew As it was neither Bought or sold No Nor the least mention made of it Either by word or writing, Moreover No other purchaser never made the least claim of the Pew in Hexham-shire Chappel.*

Hon^d^ *Sir*

I hope you will see that <u>Pew</u> is my right by Inheritance, therefore I Humbly request you will be pleased to order your Agent there to let me and my Tennants have peaceable possession once more and the favour will be gratefully acknowledged by your Faithfull Friend and Humble servant

Hexham 13 July 1802

Thomas Stokoe.

In 1802 Thomas Stokoe had Mire House, an allotment consisting of 5 acres and 3 stints. He sold a tenement in 1810 called Randelsheel in Hexhamshire to John Curry for £430. Although buried at St Mary's Catholic Church, a plaque in Hexham Abbey is inscribed: *'In Memory of Thomas Stokoe of Hexham, Surgeon, who died July 14*^th^ *aged 53'.*

SALE OF WORK & EXHIBITION 1916

A sale of work and exhibition was held on Saturday last, in a field kindly lent for the occasion by W. A. Blackburn, Esq., High Staples, in aid of the church funds, and a parish piano for St. Helen's, Whitley Chapel. The early part of the day did not look very propitious, but after dinner the sun seemed to come to the aid of the efforts of the choir and working party, organised by Mrs W. A. Blackburn, and with a fine day, a fairly large and representative gathering from the shire and surrounding districts made the sale a complete success.

In the unavoidable absence of the Vicar, the Rev. J. Robson (vicar of All Saints, South Shields), who has been officiating during the former's holidays, took the chair, and, in an able speech, described the objects of the sale, and then introduced Mrs Robson, who formally opened the sale, and wished it every success.

The entries for the exhibitions were large and very good. Appended are the awards of the judges, Miss D. Forster, Walls Farm, and Mrs Robson:-

Butter (confined class). – 1. Miss M. Henderson, Lee; 2. Mrs J. Sanderson, Low Eshells; 3. Miss N. Tailford, Tenter House.

Butter (open). – 1. Miss Pickering, Acton; 2. Miss Cowing, Embley; 3. Miss H. L. Lowdon, Riddlehamhope.

Bread (brown). – 1. Miss Lambert, Slaley; 2. Mrs J. Teasdale, Lee; 3. Miss Johnson, Stotsfold.

Bread (white). – 1. Miss A. Forster, Smelting Syke; 2. Miss M. Pigg, Raw Green; 3. Mrs Huddleston, Dye House.

Eggs (brown). – 1. Mrs Jos. Teasdale, Dukesfield; 2. Mrs Henderson, Hamburn Hall.

Eggs (white). – 1. Mrs Pigg, Raw Green; 2. Miss Atkin, High Staples.

Needlework – 1. Miss Bell, Raw Green; 2. Miss M. Pigg, Raw Green; 3. Miss Robertson, Hexham; 4. Miss Rutherford.

A writing competition was held for the three schools in Hexhamshire, and the adjudicator, Mr J. Pickop of Bagraw, in his report says: - "The writing is very creditable, and competitions of this kind help to promote greater interest in the subject, and a better understanding and more sympathy between the children, parents, and teachers." Results:-

Senior boys (over 10 years). – 1. H. Jewitt, Ordley School; 2. W. N. Swallow, Ordley School.

Junior boys. – 1. Wm. Scott, Ordley School; 2. Robt. Oliver, Ordley School.

Senior girls (over 10 years). – 1. M. Nixon, Lilswood School; 2. N. Clark, Whitley School.

Junior girls. – 1. H. Patrick, Lilswood School; 2. E. Simpson, Ordley School.

The stalls for the sale of goods were under the superintendence of: -

No. 1, Mrs W. A. Blackburn and Mrs R. Parnaby. No. 2, Miss Hughes and Miss Johnson, Dotland Park.

The bread cutting and tea infusing were under the able management of the Misses Cowing, Scott, Nichol, and M. Cowing, whilst the tea-tables were gracefully presided over by Misses Dixon, Craggs, Johnson, Pigg, Charlton, etc.

During the sale selections of music were rendered by the choir and Mrs Tindale, Monkseaton, and Miss Little, Black Hall.

The committee desires to tender thanks to all the donors of goods or money, those who assisted in erecting tents, or aided on day of sale, and especially to the judges, Mrs Robson, Miss D. Forster, and Mr J. Pickop, for all the trouble and care they took in adjudicating the numerous entries.

Hexham Courant   September 16th 1916

SCHOOLING AT ST HELEN'S CHURCH

A chapel building on the site of St. Helen's church appears to have been used for schooling from at least the 16th century.

'There had been in old times a little chapel, dedicated to St. Helen, commonly called Whitley chapel, which had been entirely ruin'd and rebuilt by subscriptions sometime before the restoration c1660 to teach school; and the neighbourhood to meet upon occasion'.

1662   June 18th 'I am content to give out of the intacks of the middle and high quarter of Hexham Shire, the sum of three pounds yearly, for the use of a schoolmaster at Whitley Chapel' William Fenwick

1699   William Rumney was the schoolmaster. He married Mary Gerard on March 10th 1699 at Hexham. Their daughter Sarah was baptised at Hexham on March 6th 1701, while Rumney was still schoolmaster.

1764   As was usual practice the curate or local preacher would provide schooling at the church. As Rev. Abraham Brown had been appointed Whitley's first perpetual curate, he will have undertaken these duties.
When Brown died in 1812 aged 92, he left the interest on £120 to support a schoolmaster. In 1830 it was noted that this paid for the education of five children.

1834   Wilson Bell became master of Whitley Chapel school on November 22nd .

1836   Joseph Dixon of Dukesfield Hall was elected clerk of the chapel on May 28th. Diarist Thomas Dixon records on June 5th . 'At the re-opening of the Chapel, my father was clerk'. As clerk his responsibilities included the church school as Thomas often referred to his father 'being at school'. His entry for September 23rd states 'Father broken up the school for Harvest'. This important period in the farming year required the children to help get the crops and hay in. 'Father began school again' on October 9th.

1850   A purpose built National School, with a schoolhouse, was opened opposite the church in this year. This was to be supported by the Church of England but built by donations of work and materials from local people. The school was enlarged in 1881 at the cost of £160.

THE CURATES OF ST HELEN'S CHURCH

1618   Richard Parker is recorded as curate of Hexhamshire.

1718   Robert Foster became the new church warden.

1742   Thomas Hudson, Master of Hexham Grammar School, was also appointed curate of Whitley and Blanchland. He was dismissed or resigned in early 1747 following complaints from Hexhamshire residents who objected to his lack of interest in his congregation and his rare attendance at the church.

1747   Abraham Brown, Master of Hexham Grammar School, 'does duty every Sunday, for a very small Salary'. He was licensed by the Archbishop of York on 26th August 1765 on the nomination of Sir Walter Blackett.
Rev. Brown was the first Perpetual Curate of Whitley Chapel and was minister of the chapel for 60 years, residing at Mollersteads from 1764.

1813   Rev. John Hewitson was licensed by the Archbishop of York. His sub-curate Rev. Richard Close, resident at Mollersteads, appears to have been responsible for all church duties as Rev. Hewitson never ministered at Whitley other than on the day of his 'reading in'. Rev. Close died on March 13th 1834 and is buried at Slaley.

1834   H. Nanney was the new incumbent at St Helen's.

1841 Rev. William Sisson was vicar of St Helen's for 65 years and vicar of Slaley St Mary's for 52 years. Rev. Sisson and his wife Elizabeth are buried in St Helen's churchyard.
Curate J Cutting signed registers on behalf of Rev Sisson from 1902 - 1906.

1906 Rev. Arthur Lees. A commemorative inset marble plaque in the church was erected by parishioners.

1916 No vicar, so registers were signed by J H Salisbury as 'acting vicar' until 1918.

1919 Rev. Stanley Claude Bryson. A newly enlarged house at Whitley Mill, previously known as Whitley Cottage, became the new Vicarage. Extensions were completed around 1924.
 Rev. Bryson was also chaplain to the Wooley Sanitorium from 1925.

1927 Rev. R Livesey
1932 Rev. Clement C Fox
1937 Rev. H Pastle
1940 Rev. John R Davison
1944 Rev. O E Hall

1949 Rev. William Dunsmore Lee. Rev. 'Billy' Lee and family are commemorated with a cross in the churchyard. He was 80 when he died in October 1990.

1976 Rev. Peter Moore

1987 Canon Anthony Duncan, who wrote many books on religion and was an accomplished poet and musician. A commemorative window was installed in the church in 2004.

1996 Rev. Andrew Patterson

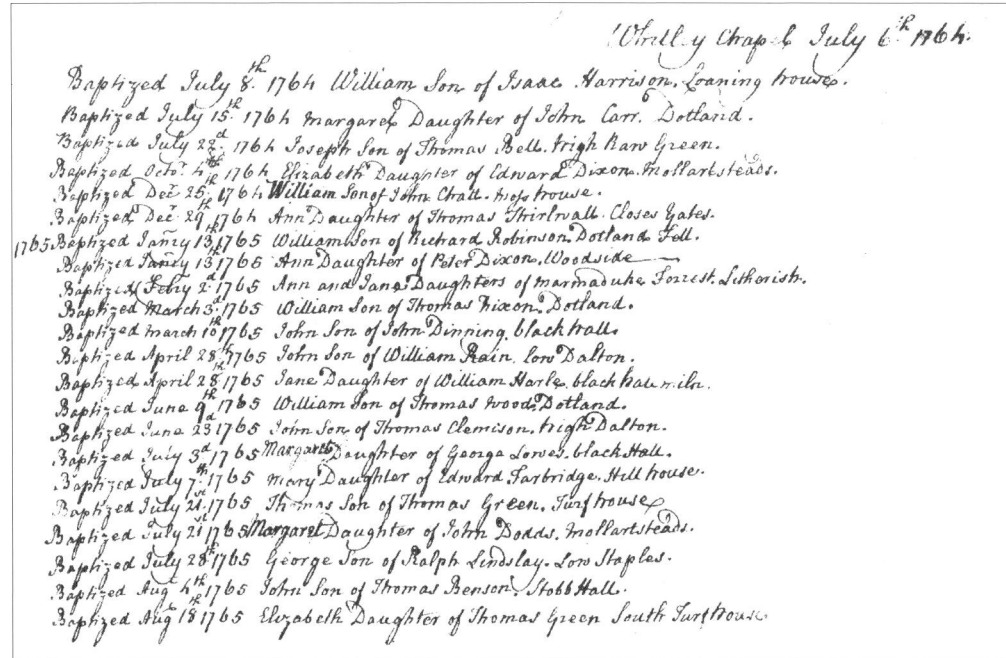

The first page of Rev. Abraham Brown's baptisms register.

St Helen's Church, Whitley, Hexhamshire
WILL BE
RE-OPENED
AFTER RESTORATION,
On FRIDAY, November 25th, 1910
AT 2·30 P.M.,
PREACHER :—
The Right Reverend LORD BISHOP of NEWCASTLE
OFFERTORY FOR THE DIOCESAN SOCIETY.
TEA will be provided in the School after the Service, at 1s. each.
A SOCIAL will be held in the School during the Evening Admission, 6d. each, including Refreshments.

REVEREND ABRAHAM BROWN

November 26th 1720 - Abraham Brown was baptized at Watermillock, Cumberland, son of James Brown and Dorothy (nee Slee).
October 1745 - Brown was ordained at St Cuthbert's Church, Corsenside where his father was curate.
May 11th 1747 - Appointed Master of Hexham Grammar School.
June 23rd 1747 - Married Alice Dixon of Slaley at St Giles church, Chollerton.
1748 - Acting as curate at Whitley Chapel.
August 26th 1765 - Licensed by Archbishop of York
1764 - Appointed first perpetual Curate at Whitley Chapel
1774 - Brown was clerk for the Poll Book & Electoral Register (Tynedale Ward).

Whilst Brown was Master at the Grammar School he would have resided at the Master's house attached to the school. Around the time that the new house at Mollersteads was built he was appointed Curate at Whitley and apparently left the grammar school and moved to the Shire.

Alice Brown died January 4th 1780, aged 79 years.

Mrs Hannah Angus, of Juniper Dye House, comments in her 1780 diary:
'Jan'ry 3rd Mrs Brown of Mollersteads very ill'
'Jan'ry 5th Only got news of poor Mrs Brown's death yesterday'
'Jan'ry 6th Nanny gone to Mollersteads to help Mrs Ord with ye burial'

Abraham Brown died November 8th 1812, aged 92 years. Engraved on his headstone, above his wife Alice's name, are the words 'Here lies all that was mortal of THE REVEREND ABRAHAM BROWN upwards of 60 years Minister of Whitley Chapel and its first Perpetual Curate.' He was buried on November 11th.

Abraham and Alice had no living children so Abraham left his estate, 'goods & chattels' to his many friends and relatives. Rev. Brown was well loved amongst his parishioners. In his will he had made provision for them –

'To the Poor of the said Chapelry of Whitley the sum of six pounds' and 'the Interest or Dividends of one hundred pounds part thereof to the Poor belonging to the Chapelry of Whitley and the Interest or Dividends of the residue thereof to a Schoolmaster for teaching of five children'.

THE VICARAGE AT MOLLERSTEADS

plate 6

Left-
Although Mollersteads, dating from at least the 16th century, already consisted of several buildings, a new house was built which was considered more appropriate for the new vicar.

Below-
Juniper House was later used as a vicarage in additon to Slaley vicarage.

The Mollersteads estate was purchased in 1764 in order to provide an income to maintain St Helen's church and to support its own curate. It was sold by the heirs of John Thirlwall who had lived at Woodside (part of Mollersteads estate, later the Fox and Hounds). Thirlwall died in 1756 at the age of 17.

In 1764 the purchase price of £500 had been agreed but at the last minute the price was increased to £1,000. The situation was saved by

Sir Walter Blackett, who generously doubled his promised contribution and purchased the estate outright of September 18th 1764.

To Rev. Dr Sharp at Hartburn
'The purchase of Mollersteads is now completed and I shall be very glad to have full instructions from you how this Estate is intended to be settled upon Whitley Chapel; and I will give instructions for drawing the writings.' [7]
Henry Richmond, agent to Sir Walter Blackett

plate 7

THE GALLERY &
CHURCH MUSIC

Dorothy Johnson of Dotland Park wrote, in the mid 20th century, about the chapel in her W. I. article 'This was my Village':

"Grandparents told us about Hexhamshire in the 19th century, Whitley Chapel (ill-lighted and earthern floored) had a gallery and fiddlers".

A gallery would have been installed at the west end of St Helen's around 1743 when the church was completely rebuilt.

The choir members, usually male, sang psalms unaccompanied, making a welcome change from the spoken word. It was not long before the introduction of hymns and the inclusion of various musical instruments such as violins, fiddles, cellos, clarinets and flutes made further use of the west end galleries in country parish churches.

Often a single musician would lead a group of singers for certain pieces of music. The congregation would be led by the choir who were considered a vital part of the service.

Some churches maintained their musicians' instruments by paying for strings and reeds. The cost of purchasing their own copies of the various tune books was often too expensive for the musicians so they would buy one copy and carefully copy the music into their own books.

plate 8

plate 9

One Shire musician did just that: *'Edward George Dinning's Book of Music, Lillswood, February 14th 1857'* consists of numerous psalm and hymn tunes, all neatly written on the manuscript pages. Other names added later to the tune book include J Dinning, Matthew Stobbs and Alexander Munroe.

Edward was born on September 20th 1840, the son of John and Margery Dinning (nee Johnson) who were living at Low Lilswood at this time. John was a farmer and lead smelter whilst Margery was a shopkeeper and grocer at the time of the 1851 & 1861 censuses.

Edward married Elizabeth Hook in 1873. He was a widower by 1880 after his third child was born. By the late 1890s he had been appointed the Master of Haltwhistle's Workhouse and died on June 11th 1919.

THE SHIRE SINGING SCHOOL

Singing Masters would travel around an area teaching singing; they charged for their tuition and often supplied sheet music.

There was a singing school set up at St Helen's in 1831 according to diarist Thomas Dixon:

1831

Sunday 31ˢᵗ July *"Chapel afternoon with my fiddle"*

Tuesday 4ᵗʰ October *"Armstrong begun a singing school at Chapel last night"*

Tuesday 25ᵗʰ October *"At Chapel singing at night"*

Sunday 30ᵗʰ October *"At Chapel; sung Jubilate for first time – the singing master here"*

Wednesday 23ʳᵈ November *"At Chapel singing at night"*

Sunday 11ᵗʰ December *"At Chapel singing at night"*

1832

Thursday 19ᵗʰ January *"Armstrong singing master here to tea – At Chapel singing at night the last night for the Master"*

Thomas apparently started to teach the singing:

Friday 20ᵗʰ January *"Teaching singing at night"*

Saturday 21ˢᵗ January *"Writeing tunes for the scholars"*

Saturday 7ᵗʰ July *"Writeing John Dixon the Jubilate"*

Thursday 1ˢᵗ November *"Writeing tune from John Thompson's book"*

1834

Sunday 10ᵗʰ August *"At the Chapel with Jane [his wife] hearing Mr Nanne preach his first sermon"*

Sunday 7ᵗʰ September *"At Chapel meeting - the Shire Head singers"*

Thursday 2ⁿᵈ October *"Harry Armstrong begun a singing school at the Chapel"*

Friday 10ᵗʰ October *"Hearing Harry's singers at night"*

Saturday 18ᵗʰ October *At Chapel singing"*

Friday 24ᵗʰ October *"Todd and I at the singing school"*

1836

Sunday 25ᵗʰ June *"At Chapel with Joe: sung the "Heavenly Vision & "Lift up your Heads"*

1841

Saturday 25ᵗʰ December *"Had our grand festival at the Chapel"*

By the latter part of the 19ᵗʰ century gallery music was becoming unfashionable and with the purchase of a new harmonium around 1868 the days of the gallery choir and musicians were numbered. There was a lot of bad feeling about this new acquisition and when the new *1861 Hymns, Ancient & Modern* books replaced the hand transcribed tune books, the musicians were no longer needed in their church.

Thomas Hardy makes references in *Under the Greenwood Tree*, written in 1872, in regard of this period.

After Reuben asked for the choir to be given *"a little time, and not be done away wi' till Christmas"*, the vicar explains *"Well, what I want you all to understand that I have no personal fault to find, and that I don't wish to change the church music by forcible means, or in a way which should hurt the feelings of any parishioners ...... and as the organ I brought with me is here waiting, there is no reason to delay"*

'Fancy proceeded to the church. The organ stood at one side of the chancel, close to and under the immediate eye of the vicar when he was in the pulpit, and also in full view of the congregation. Here she sat down, for the first time in this conspicuous position, her seat having been in a remote spot in the aisle.

The old choir, with humbled hearts, no longer took their seats in the gallery as heretofore, but were scattered about with their wives in different parts of the church. Having nothing to do with conducting the service for almost the first time in their lives they all felt awkward, out of place, abashed, and inconvenienced by their hands.'

plate 10

The Church Choir c.1922

Back Row, from left: Mr Parnaby (schoolmaster), Matt Cowing
Middle Row: Rev. Bryson, Archie Scott, Miss Dorothy Johnson, (Dotland Park), Mrs Blackburn (High Staples), Mrs Pigg (Raw Green),
Mildred Cowing (later Mrs Nixon), Michael Gibson.
Front Row: Miss Elizabeth Johnson (Dotland Park), Miss Winifrid Southern (later Mrs Syd White), Miss Hughes (Whitley Chapel schoolteacher),
Miss Bella Johnson (daughter of coachman at Stotsfold Hall), Miss Annie Johnson (Dotland Park), later Mrs Ellis Pickworth.

THE FUNERAL OF
Rev. WILLIAM SISSON

On Saturday there were laid to rest the mortal remains of the time honoured, well-beloved Vicar of Slaley and Whitley Chapel. Born of a sturdy Westmorland family at Orton on 2nd June 1816, he far outlived his own generation. Of a clerical family throughout, he had been sent in the thirties to the University of Durham, when he obtained the L.Th. in the days when this diploma ranked practically as a degree in divinity. In 1841 he was appointed Vicar of Whitley, in Hexhamshire. This living was very small in stipend, and in 1854 the parish of Slaley almost equally small and precarious in stipend, was added to it. Until the end he remained the vicar of the united parishes, but left them in a much better financial position. His long pastorate as parish priest had been such that he was in very truth the father of his people. None needing sympathy failed to come and lay their burden of trouble before him, and found ever in him the keenest interest and the clearest advice. His intellectual and spiritual faculties remained clear and perfect up to the last. In the very last hour of his sojourn, the prayers and collects of his church were entered into with full warmth and earnestness.

There lies outside the ancient village of Slaley a little well of clear cold water which in earlier days was considered to bear healing properties, and was known as the Traking Well. Over 60 years before, when he first came into the village, the first thing offered to him was a drink from the Traking Well. He never lost his love for the clear old spring. Like David in the camp longing for the well of Bethlehem, in his last hour he craved a drink of the Traking Well, and this was his last

nourishment before he passed calmly to "where beyond these voices there is peace."

It was a quaint and pathetic sight on Saturday afternoon to see the long line of carriages and traps of every description which followed the village hearse along the country lane from Slaley Vicarage to Whitley Chapel, three miles away. It was an ideal summer's day. "All the air a solemn stillness held," flooded with golden sunlight, which spoke of the noble life quietly led in doing its duty among the kind-hearted folk of the "Shire" and Slaley. From far away Shepherd Farm, from Blackburn to Lilswood, from Dotland to The Steel, they gathered to see the worn out warrior laid in his resting place beside the remains of the wife who passed before him 30 years ago. He sleeps on the slope of

Whitley Chapel Yard where it overlooks the sweet valley of Devilswater, where in earlier days he had sometimes found a dish of speckled trout for the breakfast of his sick parishioners, and away fell after fell right up Hexhamshire, where he had often visited the hill shepherds and lead miners that once upon a time so thickly populated Hexhamshire. He would often speak of how the population has gradually shrunk like the rest of rural England.

Hexham Courant   July 1906

Rev. William Sisson died July 17th 1906, aged 90. Elizabeth, his wife, died May 20th 1876, aged 52. Their headstone was erected in churchyard at east end of church.

THE CHURCHYARD

The old chapel at Whitley had no place of burial for its inhabitants until 1752 when the Lord of the Manor granted a parcel of land to the church-wardens *'William Dixon of Harwood Sheel, William Armstrong of Nether-Raw-green, Joseph Dodd of the Lee and George Bell of Hackford'* as tenants to be used as a *'Chapel yard or burying place'* for 1d per annum.

'A piece or parcel of Common or Waste Ground at or near Whitley Chapel in Hexhamshire within the said Manor containing one hundred yards or thereabouts from North to South and eighty yards or thereabouts from East to West, boundering on the High Road on the North side of the said Chapel on or towards the North, a wall near the said Chapel on or towards the South, the Hedge of the grounds of John Johnson called Chapel-Row'. [8]

However in 1759 when the churchyard had still not been consecrated a petition was addressed to the Lord Archbishop of York from churchward-ens and parishioners of the High and Middle Quarters of Hexhamshire.
George Sparke represented the Middle Quarter with John Johnson, Thomas Farbridge, Thomas Johnson, Jonathan Ward, William Ord, William Angus, Thomas Williamston, Thomas Clemison, Jonathan Nattrass, Joseph Ward, George Sparke; Robert Ward represented the High Quarter with John Armstrong, Thomas Ridley, Robert Forster, Matthew Carr and John Ord.

'We want to have the said Chappel consecrated in order to bury our dead … some of us being twelve miles from Hexham which is very hard upon us especially in the winter season when the

plate 11   1920

days are short and the roads is bad we have to come home in the night some time at eleven or twelve o'clock at night'. [9]

As no consecration had taken place by February 1763 another petition was submitted.
Thomas Bell, Thomas Ridley and John Ellerington, churchwardens of the High, Middle and Low Quarters informed the Lord Archbishop of York that *'The inhabitants usually resort to the Chapel to attend publick worship, but are obliged to bury their Dead at the Mother Church [Hexham] which distresses them greatly at all Times, more especially in Winter when the Roads, which are always inaccessible to Carriages, are worse in Proportion to the Severity of the Season and sometimes rendered impassable by the overflow-ing of two or three rapid Rivulets. Inconveniences now and then arise from this last Circumstance, and a Corpse was stopt not long ago by the sudden swelling of the aforesaid Brooks'.* [10]

On August 25th 1763 Archdeacon Sharp, in a letter to the Lord Archbishop of York, comments on the people of the area –
'No doubt a Tract on Confirmation will be of great service to the Inhabitants, especially the younger part of them. The miners in general, with which that part of the Country abounds, are a much more decent set of people than the Colliers, & many of them come tolerably well to Church'.

Eventually the parishioners' prayers were answered when the Lord Archbishop held a confirmation at the church on July 6th 1764 and consecrated the churchyard. The churchyard was extended in 1946 and again in 2011.
The yew trees would have been planted in the early days of the church. These evergreen long-lived trees were considered sacred by ancient Britons and were thought to guard against evil.

HEADSTONES & BURIALS

Rev. Abraham Brown began his beautifully written parish registers in 1764, the first burial being that of John Maughan of Mollersteads on July 19th. Although the churchyard was only consecrated that year, a few burials had already taken place according to the Hexham burial registers.

In the 250 years since 1764 around 3000 burials have taken place in the Whitley Chapel churchyard. Over 350 headstones stand in the old and new yards in commemoration of Hexhamshire families: the vast majority of burials having no identification or markers. The high cost of erecting an engraved headstone would have been beyond most families; a wooden cross may have marked the grave for a limited period. Depending on where they lived some Shire residents may have been buried at Allendale, Hunstanworth, Blanchland, Slaley or Hexham, particularly before 1764. In a few instances small burial areas would be near to their dwellings: Riddlehamhope and Halliwell are recorded as having their own ancient burial plots.

The funerals of the better off members of the community may have been extremely expensive depending on the requirements of the family of the deceased. In a list of funeral expenses for Mrs Mary Robson, from 1785, the *'strong elm coffin covered with fine black finished handsome with 2 Rows nails, three pairs of large handles & large plate, all japan'd Black, the inside lin'd with fine crepe ruffled & pitched'* cost £2 18 0d. Amongst the many other expenses, the hire of a *'Velvet Pall'* to cover the coffin cost 10s, five pairs of black silk gloves, 15s 6d, and a *'Grave digger for extra deep grave, 1s.'*

Hannah Angus wrote about the funeral of Rev. Abraham Brown's wife, Alice Brown, in her diary entry for January 7th 1780 that *'My Hus and Nanney [their daughter] at ye burial. It was a very grand one, everyone got hatbands & gloves.'*

In Thomas Dixon's diary there are several mentions of members of the community getting together to 'make cakes' before funerals to cater for the mourners:

Richard Tweddle's list of coffins made in the 1880s:

Mrs Jane Little, Harwood Shield	[died May 25th 1882, aged 65]
Mrs Mary White, Westburnhope	[died May 18th 1883, aged 77]
Mrs Ann White, Rowley Head	[died January 3rd 1883, aged 45]
Jane Pigg, Rowley Head	[died August 1st 1882, aged 29]
Mrs Margaret Pigg, Rowley Head	[died October 2nd, 1881, aged 69]
Hannah Broom, Burnt Ridge	[no burial at Whitley found]
Sarah Tamar Elliott, Burnt Ridge	[buried May 6th 1883, aged 1]
Sarah Jane Elliott, nee Bright, Burnt Ridge,	[mother of above, died 1883?]
John James,	[buried August 3rd 1882, aged 7]
Ann Magee, Literidge	[buried January 27th 1884, aged 67]
Thomas Scott, Heigh	[died October 6th 1884, aged 78]
William Scott, Heigh	[died January 20th 1886, aged 85]
Margaret Routledge, Longlee	[buried September 6th 1885, aged 39]
Elizabeth Robson, Hesleywell	[buried May 12th 1885, aged 82]
Nanney Hutchinson, Longlee	[buried November 26th 1884, aged 80]
Oliver Hutchinson, Longlee	[buried September 14th 1886, aged 55]
William Stokoe, Rawgreen	[died November 25th 1884, aged 79]
Thomas Oxley, Rawgreen	[no burial at Whitley found]
Margaret Roddam, Rawgreen	[died March 30th 1886, aged 35]
Hannah Carr, Garshield	[buried December 29th 1882, aged 17]
John Oliver, Dotland	[died November 7th 1884, aged 25]
John Charlton, Intack	[buried March 26th 1885, aged 8 months]
Hannah Charlton, Juniper	[buried January 24th 1886, aged 78]
Dorothy Anderson,	[died July 13th 1883, aged 16]
Dorothy Stobbs	[buried May 30th, 1884, aged 30]

Joiner & Cartright Richard Tweddle of Rawgreen made coffins in addition to general repairs and building work.

Thursday 30th July 1838 "Sister Sarah departed this life at half past nine at night".
Saturday 1st August "Went to Dukesfield with the 2 Janes [his wife & daughter], the cakes made"
Sunday 2nd August "Sarah's funeral today".

The churchyard is a fascinating source of historical information: many headstones, some dating from the late 1700s, give family names, ages and dates in addition to recording their dwellings.

Five headstones have English Heritage grade II listing for historical interest:

The earliest is that of John Curry of Gairshield, erected in 1773, which also includes his widow Mildred and sons Matthew and Thomas.

Rev. Abraham Brown and his wife Alice share an 1812 headstone, with an intricately carved upper area. It can be found outside the east end of the church.

Two headstones near to each other, to the south side of the church, commemorate the Carr family of Dotland Park (1831) and Thomas and Elizabeth Adamson of Spitalshield (1860).

The fifth, and most recent, is the 1917 Northumberland Fusiliers headstone inscribed to Private J W Simpson, from Juniper.

1. John Curry and family
2. Rev. Abraham Brown and wife Alice
3. Thomas and Elizabeth Adamson
4. Private J. W. Simpson

Looking at the ages of the buried, it would seem that those who survived childhood might expect a reasonably long life. According to the burial registers between 1812 and 1953 around 30 'Shire inhabitants were over 90 years old when they died.

Whilst Robert Stokoe would not now be considered elderly, 27 year old diarist Thomas Dixon writes that *'Old Robt. Stokoe died'* on September 6th 1832. Robert, a blacksmith at Chapel House, was only 63 when he died.

The inscription on the west side of his headstone reads:

My anvil and hammers lie declin'd,
My bellows have quite lost their wind,
My fire's extinct, my forge decay'd,
My vices are in the dust all laid,
My coals are spent, my iron gone,
My nails are drove, my work is done,
My mortal part rests nigh this stone,
My soul to heaven I hope is gone.

plate 12

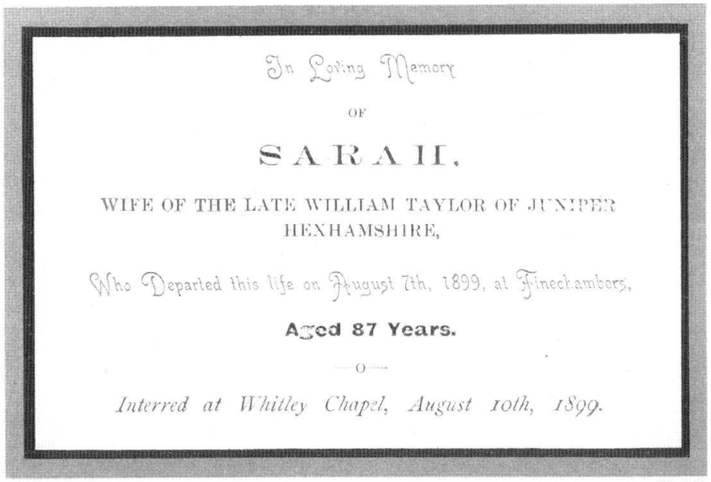

In Loving Memory

IN LOVING MEMORY.

In Loving Memory

OF

SARAH.

WIFE OF THE LATE WILLIAM TAYLOR OF JUNIPER
HEXHAMSHIRE,

Who Departed this life on August 7th, 1899, at Fineckambers,

Aged 87 Years.

—o—

Interred at Whitley Chapel, August 10th, 1899.

In Loving Memory

Left and above - Remembrance cards such as these were circulated amongst mourners to commemorate the funeral and life of the deceased.

Near left - The 19th century church with the hearse house in the foreground.

Below - An example of funeral expenses in 1777

Elizabeth Armstrong's Funeral Expenses; she died on November 27th 1777, the daughter of Richard Ord of Nether Ardley.

Coffin	10 – 10 - 0
Church Fees	0 - 10 - 8
Underbearers	0 - 8 - 0
Cheese	0 - 9 - 7
Liquor	2 - 10 -11
Miss Donaldson for mourning [clothes]	5 - 17 -10
Mr Charlton ditto	23 - 12 - 0
Mr Scott's Expenses Horse hire	1 - 17 - 6
	£46 – 11 - 7

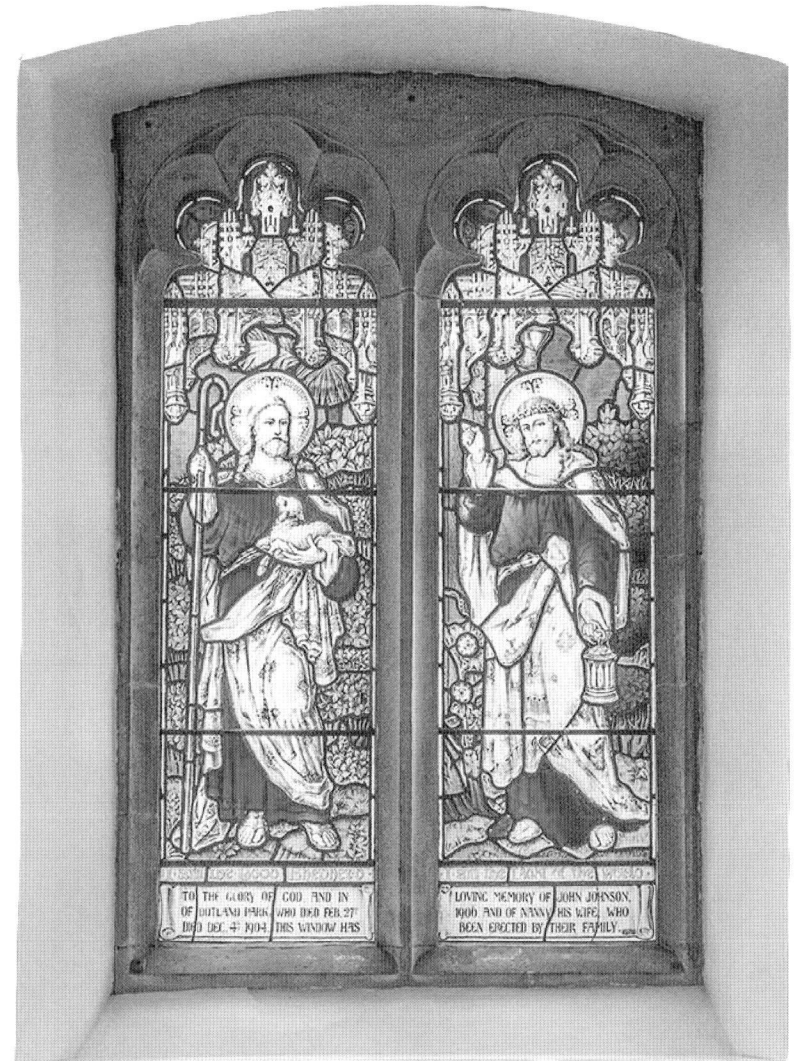

Stained glass window erected in memory of John and Nanny Johnson of Dotland Park.

plate 13

Charity Begins at Home

The Poor Law Act of 1601 made parishes responsible for their own poor. Requests for financial assistance were dealt with by the parish or brought before the Quarter Sessions, held in the case of the Shire, at Hexham's Moot Hall.
A local tax, often called 'poor cess' was raised from all householders within the parish based on the value of their property. If the Justices of the Peace were convinced by an appeal for aid, an order stating how much money had been granted was taken back to the parish officers to administer. This was the system known as 'out relief', and paupers could stay in their own homes.
In 1834, The Poor Law Amendment Act saw a change from 'out-relief' to 'indoor relief' - the workhouse system. The responsibility for looking after the poor of the 'Shire community was transferred to the newly built Hexham Work House in 1839.

Quarter Sessions
Midsummer at Hexham 1712

Petition for Poverty

"To the Right Worshipful Her Majesty's Justices of the Peace for the County of Northumberland.

Humbly sheweth that whereas Ann Bell wife of John Bell, Skinner, who served his time in Hexham, and was made free, and after he had spent his own and that of the petitioner had (which she lived very well on without being troublesome to any of her neighbours) took on in the Queen's Service, and left her in a deplorable condition as was formerly showen when she received an absolute order for one shilling in the week from the 19th of July 1711 which she hath not received.

Dalton

Therefore your poor petitioner begs of the honourable Bench that she may have the remainder paid, and then that it may be paid monthly after. And your petitioner shall Daily pray."

Rejected

11

Quarter Sessions
Midsummer at Hexham 1712

Petition for Poverty

"To the Right Worshipful Her Majesty's Justices of the Peace for the County of Northumberland, The Humble Petition of Barbara Errington spinster, Humbly sheweth

That your petitioner (a daughter of Robert Errington) was born at the Barker House in the Middle Quarter of Hexham Shire is so sick and lame and weak that she is not able to work (or go about the country to beg) and therefore Humbly prays the Worshipful Bench would be pleased to grant her an order for a certain weekly allowance to be paid out of the said Division towards her maintenance.

And your petitioner as in duty bound shall ever pray.

Rejected

12

Quarter Sessions
Midsummer at Hexham 1712

To the Honorable Bench

The Petition of Ann Turner
of Hexhamshire in the Same
Countey widdow

Humbly

*Showeth that Your Petitioner is a very poor
& decrepid woman aged Eighty Two years not
able to doe any thing towards the winning of
a life and by reason of the great Imperfection
in her eyes occasioned through old agescarce
able to discern the highway or to goe from one
neighbours house to another to crave the Almes
of well disposed persons, And having most of
her time lived credibly by honest Endeavours
was loth to be troublesome but that Extream
poverty compels her to beg assistance without
which she will undoubtedly starve having noe
dependance but what of good will comes from
well disposed Christians*

*Where fore your Petitioner begs that the
honourable Bench in Consideration had to the
miserable Condition of this Real object of Pitty
to grant unto her being not able to guide her-
selfe such weekly Allowance as may by you be
thought fit towards her Reliefe & manitance
And your Petitioner
As in duty bound
shall ever pray &c*

1ˢ/6ᵈ per week

13

Quarter Sessions
Midsummer at Hexham 1713

Petition for Poverty

14

Barbara Errington eventually received the help
she was looking for in 1713.
Baptised on July 3ʳᵈ 1667; the daughter of Robert
Errington of Barker House. She died at the age of
53 and was buried at Hexham Abbey on July 22ⁿᵈ
1720; it is not known if she had been living at the
workhouse at this time.

Quarter Sessions
Hexham 1723

William Langland

*"These are to acquaint the honourable Bench
that William Langland being a poor, weak,
impotent and distressed Creature, and not able
to work or do anything through his lameness
and impotency, moved the honourable Bench
with a petition for relief out of the Parish where
he was born in the year 1721 and this honourable Bench bid him go to the parishioners and
tell them that this honourable Bench willeth you
to let William Langland have relief out of the
Parish where he was borne.*

*And he went and told the heads of the Parish,
and they all huffed at his words, and said unto
them that 'they cared neither for Justice nor
Jury, for they had a law among themselves and
no other would they obey'.
And he told them that he would return their answer to this honourable Bench and at last they
told him if he would take sixpence in the week,
they would give him that and four shillings per
annum out of the poor money that they had to
distribute yearly among the poor in that parish.*

*So the 6d per week and the 4 shillings of the
poor money makes thirty shillings – this thirty
shillings they promised to pay him per annum,
and sixpence they have paid him for a year and
a half, but they will not give him any thing of
the four shillings of the poor money which they
all did promise to give him besides the 6d per
week.*

15

continued

Therefore may it please this honourable Bench to grant him an order under the seal of the sessions that this poor object of pity may have relief out of the parish and the petitioner shall ever be bound to pray.

Hexham High Quarter: 6d per week from this time without further notice"

Quarter Sessions
Midsummer 1775

Thomas Nixon, Hexhamshire Low Quarter Yeoman & Overseer of the poor-

Refusing to obey order to give poor relief to Hannah Bennett

Fine - £5

16

'*On Monday last, a coroner's inquest was holden at Bedlington on the body of Eleanor SIMPSON, widow, aged 93. She was found burnt to death near to the fire-place in her own room, on the morning of Good Friday. Verdict – Accidental. This old woman received parochial weekly allowance. A question here naturally arises on the propriety of indulging aged paupers in their wish to live alone, and unattended, rather than go into the parish poor-house.*'

Newcastle Courant   April 8th 1820

Above - A list of tax paid by Mr Sample on behalf of Greenwich Hospital's woods in Hexhamshire, giving details of payments to the poor of the parish.

Below - Moot Hall in Hexham's market place where the Quarter Sessions were held.

plate 14

Pauper Burials

As the following were buried in Whitley churchyard at the expense
of the Parish, their burial register entries were marked *'pauper'*.
The parish owned a hearse (kept in the nearby hearse house) which
was available to all members of the community who needed it.

BELL Christopher	6-7-1789	Dotland Park Head
DIXON Jane	18-2-1793	Mollersteads
DODD Jonathon	4-2-1791	Oxen Roads
GREEN George	11-1-1789	Low Dye House
HUNTER Hannah	23-10-1793	Turf House
JOHNSON Elizabeth	16-8-1793	Nether Mirehouse
MILBURN Elizabeth	11-3-1790	Stonehouse
MILBURN Jonathon	29-12-1812	Harwood Shield
NEWTON Elizabeth	7-2-1794	Ordley
RELF Elizabeth	23-5-1793	Leemoorhouse
SCOTT Joseph	2-12-1790	West Quarter
SISTERSON Jonathon, inft.	2-9-1788	Turf House
STOBBS Eleanor	25-4-1791	Heathery Haugh
STOBERT Elizabeth	11-6-1788	Heathery Haugh
WALLIS Jane	24-7-1810	White Hall
WINTER Alice	28-3-1785	High Dalton

plate 15

Chapel House c.1910

A Benefit Concert on Behalf of Mr John Stokoe

'A concert on behalf of Mr John Stokoe, blacksmith, who is an old man and unable to work, was given in the Whitley Chapel Schoolroom on Saturday evening last.
Mr Stokoe has lived in the district during the whole of his life, and is well known and much respected, and when it was known that the concert was got up on his behalf there was no difficulty in disposing of the tickets, people being very ready to help him in time of need.
He was a worthy member of the community, and was always respected as a skillful mechanic. He was always very civil and obliging, and his charges were exceedingly moderate. He had attended his work in his shop, which was close at hand [Chapel House], for about 65 years; he went into the shop when quite a boy.
Mr Stokoe had acted as churchwarden, parish constable and overseer . . . and only forced to retire from his duties through old age and infirmities. He was wished success and every blessing for the present time and of the world to come.'

Hexham Courant   March 8th 1890

John Stokoe was buried, aged 77, on February 17th 1892; his widow Margaret, aged 76, on July 18th 1895;
both were buried in Whitley churchyard but have no headstone.

THE HEXHAM WORKHOUSE

An enormous stigma was attached to those unfortunate enough to have to enter the workhouse; it was the last resort. The elderly, chronically ill, unmarried mothers, mentally ill, orphaned children and abandoned wives usually had no alternative. The able-bodied worked in the workhouse or out in the community, returning at the end of the day. Inmates could choose to leave if they were able to find employment and somewhere to live; men finding work who could support their family had to take all their dependants with them.

1823 – '*A Poor-house is situated near the head of Priest-popple. It is a large rectangular building, and of different dates. Several poor families receive no further relief from the parish than an asylum within these walls. The person presiding over the inmates is called "the Master". He contacts for the support of the establishment, and is responsible to the Overseers for the supply of necessaries and the conduct of the persons committed to his trust.*'

After the The Hexham Poor Law Union was established on October 22nd 1836, a new Poor-Law Union Workhouse was built in 1839 at Peth Head.

The management of the workhouse was overseen by an elected Board of Governors representing the 69 parishes and townships in its constituency. There were four representatives from the 'Shire: one each from the High, Middle, Low and West Quarters.

Able-bodied men, able-bodied women, the elderly & infirm and children, as they were classified, were housed in separate areas or buildings. The dormitories usually only contained iron bedsteads with mattresses stuffed with chopped oat straw; chairs and lockers were added later but the inmates would not have had personal possessions.

Elderly married couples could be accommodated in shared bedrooms by the 1850s. For many, the workhouse would have been where the elderly and infirm spent the rest of their days.

1888 - '*The Hexham Board of Guardians expressed concerns over plans to replace bedsteads in the town's workhouse with hammocks, to make room for oakum picking.*'
Hexham Courant

Oakum picking;
the picking apart of old ropes
into their raw fibres.
'*money for old rope*'

Day rooms were sparsely furnished with tables, straight back chairs and benches. Although basic, facilities at the workhouse could occasionally be better than the homes they had left: food and shelter were always available.

Thanks to donations of books, a library was opened in 1914; newspapers and magazines would also have been available.

Clothing issued could be extremely basic: Men wore heavy jackets, trousers, striped shirts and caps whilst women wore flannel dresses, aprons, shawls and bonnets; these would have been made by those inmates with sewing and dressmaking experience.

In addition to being housed within the workhouse, 'out relief' was given to the needy in the form of food or money; this was sometimes given in return for stone-breaking or similar work.

In some cases people stayed for short periods, repeatedly entering and leaving the workhouse; these were called 'ins & outs'.

Work undertaken by the male inmates included trades such as farm work, stone masons, builders, joiners and blacksmiths; females would work as dressmakers, knitters, darners, cooks, nursery assistants and laundry women.

A Treat for the Workhouse Children

'*Yesterday, by kindness of Mrs Waddilove, Beacon Grange, the 'Wizard of the North', Mr George Robson of Liverpool, gave two hours of entertainment to the children of Hexham Workhouse, which greatly delighted his juvenile audience.*'

Hexham Courant   December 12th 1874

By 1883 extensive alterations and additions had been made, including a new dining hall, kitchens, sick wards, a porter's lodge, vagrant cells and a new house for the Master; 300 of Hexham's poorest could now be accommodated. The workhouse closed in 1939. The inmates were dispersed to Alnwick, Berwick or Morpeth institutions. The buildings became part of Hexham General Hospital.

WORK HOUSE PAINTINGS

High on the east wall in the dining room was this large framed canvas painting, approximately 10ft square, of the Royal Arms of Queen Victoria, signed 'Swinburne 1885'.

On either side and beneath the Arms are wall paintings, thought to have been painted by an Italian prisoner of war who was in the wartime hospital.

Unfortunately the wall paintings have deteriorated since these photographs were taken in 2005 but the Royal Arms canvas has been removed for restoration and conservation.

photographs by Tim Tatman

IN THE WORKHOUSE

Several Hexhamshire inhabitants are recorded as being in the Hexham workhouse for a variety of reasons: they could have been homeless, infirm or had no relatives or income. The decision to go into the workhouse would not be taken lightly.

MARY ARMSTRONG

Mrs Armstrong died at the workhouse in 1853 at the age of 78, she was buried on February 28th. Previous home unknown as only described as having lived in the High Quarter. The only Armstrong family in the 1851 census was at Riddlehamhope.

BENJAMIN ASKEW

Born in 1763, Benjamin married Dorothy Common on January 10th 1789; they lived at High Rawgreen where they brought up their four children.

Robert was baptised March 23rd 1794, Jane (named after Benjamin's mother) March 12th 1797 and twins Benjamin & John on August 3rd 1800.

Dorothy was buried on May 21st 1841 at Whitley. When Benjamin went into the workhouse is unknown but possibly around this time. Benjamin died, aged 83, in the *'poor house'* according to St Helen's burial register and was buried on November 26th 1845. There is no record to say that he had a pauper's burial.

THOMAS BRIDDOCK

In the 1851 census Thomas was living at Barker House, aged 67 and described as a pauper and agricultural labourer. He died at the workhouse, aged 74 and was buried at Hexham Abbey on February 6th 1858.

JOHN BULMAN

Unmarried and living on his own in 1851, 65 year old John was living at Dotland. He died at the workhouse on November 9th 1855 at the age of 70.

JOSEPH CARR

Baptised on May 16th 1813, the son of Thomas and Ann Carr of Dotland. Siblings George and Hannah both died in infancy; another Hannah lived until 21.

By the 1851 census, 38 year old Joseph was living with his 78 year old widowed mother Ann and 56 year old brother John at Dotland, who was a farmer of 800 acres.

There is a church entry for the burial of a Thomas Carr, aged 78, on February 26th 1836 so this was possibly Joseph's father.

By 1861 Joseph was in the workhouse, aged just 48, so Ann and John must have died by then or been unable to look after him.

JANE MATTHEWS

In the 1851 census 76 year old Jane is living at Wagtail with her grandchildren; 6 year old William Atkinson and 4 year old Anne. She is a widow and described as a pauper and agricultural labourer. Jane died in the workhouse aged 82 and was buried on November 4th 1857 at Hexham Abbey. In 1851 William and Anne's mother Margaret Atkinson was living at Dotland with a third child, 1 year old Frances. By 1861 they had moved to Helensgate, Hexham.

THOMAS TAYLOR

Baptised on October 13th 1822 at St Helen's, he was the son of carpenter William and Hannah Taylor, nee Martin, of Black Hall Smelt Mill. William was buried at Whitley, aged 57, on March 15th 1840; Hannah, aged 64, on April 18th 1850. Both were living at East/Low Smelting Syke at the time of their death.

In the 1851 census Thomas was an agricultural labourer aged 28, living with his sister and three brothers at East Smelting Syke. His uncle Robert Taylor was head of the household.

In 1881 Thomas and his unmarried 73 year old sister Mary were living at Dipton Cottages. Thomas, aged 68, was in the workhouse at the time of the 1891 census. He died at the age of 73 and was buried at Hexham Abbey on February 26th 1896.

JAMES TURNER

In the 1851 census 85 year old James was living at Barker House; a widower, pauper and agricultural labourer. He died at the workhouse in 1855 at the age of 89. James was buried at Hexham Abbey on May 11th 1855.

SARAH WINTER

Sarah was living at High Staples at the time of the 1851 census; described as a 74 year old widow, pauper and agricultural labourer. At the time of her burial at Hexham Abbey on June 27th 1858 she had been living at the workhouse.

A WOOD-CHOPPING ROOM.

plate 16

OLD WOMEN "RUSTING OUT."

plate 17

Census Returns with Pauper References

1851

BELL Frances (58), pauper (buried January 24th 1858, aged 65)	Black Hall Mill
BELL Mary (73), pauper & agricultural labourer (buried February 14th 1858, aged 79)	Dotland
BRIDDOCK Thomas (67), pauper & agricultural labourer (buried February 6th 1858, aged 74)	Barker House
CHARLTON Ann (74), widow, pauper & agricultural labourer (buried August 2nd 1852, aged 75)	Dye House
FORSTER Mary (42), pauper & agricultural labourer (buried February 5th 1879, aged 70)	Dye House
GRAHAM Robert (65), pauper, formerly farmer (buried December 18th 1852, aged 66)	Eads Bush
HUDSON Dorothy (45), pauper & quilter (buried October 17th 1887, aged 82)	Steel
MATTHEWS Jane (76), widow, pauper & agricultural labourer (buried November 4th 1857, aged 82)	Wagtail
NIXON Frances (65?), pauper (possible burial date – aged 75?, December 27th 1858)	Smelting Syke
ROBINSON Joanna (80), pauper	Dipton Cottage
ROWLAND / ROLLAND Mary (84), (buried February 12th 1857, aged 90)	Upper Lane House
STOBBS Ann (65), pauper & agricultural labourer (buried March 23rd 1869, aged 83)	Mollersteads
TURNER James (85), widower, pauper & agricultural labourer	Barker House
WAGGETT Sarah (54), pauper & labourer	Hill House

1861

ELLIOTT Ann (54), widow, pauper & agricultural labourer	
RICHARDSON Elizabeth (82), pauper & blacksmith's widow (buried December 10th 1865, aged 85)	Broadwell House

1871

DENT Margaret (62), pauper (buried December 1st 1885, aged 77)	Black Hall Mill
DODD Margaret (63), living on own means (pauper) (buried September 11th 1892, aged 72)	Litteridge Lodge
ROUTLEDGE Margaret (25), pauper, living with mother (buried September 6th 1885, aged 39)	Long Lee

It is interesting to note that in the 1881 census, the House Porter of the union workhouse was widower Walter Murray, aged 63, originally from Mire Meadows and later from Low Lane House where he was shepherd. He died at the age of 71 and was buried at Whitley on April 9th 1889.

Local Charities

Charities set up to support the poor of Hexhamshire:

1677   Robert Farbridge, of Hackforth, gave £10 to the poor of the High and Middle quarters; the interest to be distributed yearly at Whitley Chapel on All-Saints' Day.

1684   Robert Forster, of the Upper Eshells, gave £10 to the poor; the interest to be distributed yearly at Easter.

1690   Anthony Farbridge, of Newcastle, born at Hackforth, left £14 to the High and Middle quarters of the Shire; the interest to be distributed yearly on Good Friday, at Whitley Chapel.

1695   Richard Walton, of Peacock House, gave £3 towards finding a minister at Whitley Chapel; failing a minister, the interest to be distributed amongst the most needful people in the High quarter.

1702   Henry Dixon, of the Staples, gave £20 to the poor of the High, Low and Middle quarters of the Shire; the interest to be distributed yearly at Christmas.

1715   Robert Dixon directed that £20 should be placed as interest for the poor of the High and Middle Quarters, and that £10 should be paid to the minister of Whitley Chapel. If there is no minister there, the money was to be given to the poor.

1726   William Dixon left £40, the interest of which was to be given yearly to the poor in the High Quarter at Christmas and Easter.

1748   Abraham Brown gave to the poor of Whitley Chapel interest on £100 and to the schoolmaster of Whitley Chapel interest on £120.

Overseers of the Poor

Appointment of Overseers of the Poor at Hexhamshire Ratepayers Meetings:

'On Friday afternoon last a meeting of the ratepayers of the Middle Quarter was held at Woodside Inn, for the purpose of electing overseers of the poor, &c, for the ensuing year. There was a fair attendance of ratepayers, and the meeting was presided over by the Rev. W Sisson, Slaley Vicarage. Mr John Blackburn, High Staples was elected surveyor of the highways in the South Division of the quarter and Mr William Scott, Heigh, surveyor in the North Division. Mr R Stobbs, Dalton and Mr Wm Angus, Salmonfield were re-elected overseers of the poor, and Mr Wm White, Low Staples, was re-elected guardian. Mr Wm Blackburn, Steel Hall was re-elected church-warden and Mr Stokoe, Chapel House, constable.

The annual meeting of the inhabitant ratepayers of the Low Quarter, was held in the Ordley Schoolroom, on Saturday afternoon last, for the purpose of electing overseers of the poor, &c., for the ensuing year. Mr W White, Low Staples, presided, and there was a fairly good attendance. Mr G W Oliver, Dotland was elected guardian on the resignation of Councillor S Stobbs, Blackhall. Mr J Dodd, Newbiggin Hill was re-elected surveyor of the highways in the East Division of the quarter, and Mr Wm White, Low Staples, was elected surveyor of the West Division. Mr Geo Robson, Juniper, and Mr John Johnson, Dotland Park were re-elected overseers of poor, and Mr Wm Dinning, Peth Head, was elected churchwarden.'

Hexham Courant   March 30th 1889

Account of Money

Paid by John Nevin Assistant Overseer to the Out & In Paupers of Allendale Parish

These two women were supported by Allendale Parish as *'Out Paupers'* ; they were the liability of that parish, having been born there:

Elizabeth Hunter from Hexhamshire –
Allowance - 52 weeks at 1s 6d, October 8th 1824,   £4 2s 0d

Hannah Mitcheson from Harwoodshield –
Allowance – 52 weeks at 1s 6d, December 3rd 1824,   £3 18s 0d

Elizabeth Hunter, aged 82, was buried on February 28th 1825 at Whitley.
Hannah Mitcheson, aged 80, was buried on December 13th 1833 at Whitley.

Life after the Workhouse

Isabella Rutherford was listed as an inmate of the Hexham Union Workhouse in the 1881 census, an unmarried 23 year old farm servant. Her 4 year old son John James Rutherford and his 9 month old sister Jane Isabella Rutherford were born in the workhouse.

Isabella was born on June 27th 1858 at Lord's Lot, Hexhamshire. Her mother, also called Isabella, married Joseph Dixon in 1866. Although she had moved with her family to the Carlisle area, daughter Isabella had returned to Hexham by 1877 as her son John James was born on March 12th at the workhouse; she would have to have gone to Hexham as she would only receive parish relief from her town of birth.

It would seem that Isabella was employed, outside of the workhouse, as a domestic servant for coalminer Joseph Christer, a widower who lived with his children at Mickley Square. A certificate, dated February 17th 1883, records the wedding of Joseph and Isabella at Hexham.

A Happy Ending!

(Isabella's daughter, Jane Isabella Rutherford, born in 1880, married William Stobart in 1906 in Hexham. William worked as a green grocer for the co-op at Prudhoe.)

William and Jane Stobart   plate 18

Lord's Lot

School Days

WHITLEY CHAPEL

A school had been run at St Helen's church for centuries before the National School at Whitley Chapel was built in 1849 on land acquired in 1848 from T. W. Beaumont Esq. of Bywell Hall. A list of subscribers started in 1849: £286..11..4d was collected with an additional £13..8..10d in 1850. The school was in use for over 120 years. A new school building nearby was opened in 1974.

To The Right Worsp[ll.] Henry Walkinson Doctor of & Chancellor of Yorke

These are to certify yo[r] Worsp & all others whom [it] concern: That Abraham Teasdale of Dalton in Hexham Shire in the parish of Hexham & County of Northumberland & Diocese of Yorke. Is A sober pious young man of a good life & conversation conform-able to the Doctrine, Discipline of y[e] Church of England as by Law establish[ed] and is well affected to the p[r] sent Goverm[t] & every way qualifyd to teach a petty school. And these desire he may be Licenced to teach a petty school at Whitley Chapple in Hexhamshire aforesaid. As Witnesse my hand this 25th day of September Ao Dmi. 1707

George Ritschel Minister of Hexham
17   *20 Oct. 1707*

Robert Petty, aged 43, was appointed the first schoolmaster on 27th December 1849. In addition to his salary he had the schoolhouse rent free. The school opened for the first time on January 14th 1850. By 1852, 44 boys and 16 girls were attending although there was space for 70 pupils.

EXTRACTS FROM THE SCHOOL GOVERNORS' MINUTE BOOK 1849 - 1903

1852
'Hours of teaching – Morning, from 9am to 12. Afternoon, from 1.30 pm to 4.30 pm, in Summer & from 1 pm to 4 pm in Winter.
Holidays –
The Easter vacation to be the Thursday next before Good Friday till the Wednesday in Easter Week. The Summer vacation to be three weeks in the Harvest. The Christmas vacation to be a clear fortnight from the Thursday next before Christmas day.
Scholars attending the school within the period from 15th October to the 15th April following, to pay 6d each for fuel for the schoolroom.'

1852
John James was appointed the new schoolmaster on May 13th; his wife as schoolmistress. When they resigned in 1857, they were replaced by Alexander Falconer and his wife.

1866
An inventory includes 1 stove, 4 fixed desks, 3 fixed forms, 5 loose forms, blackboard with stand, 36 books on various subjects such as geography, writing, algebra, household matters, reading books for female schools, grammar, money matters and agriculture. The teacher's salary was £55..11..6d.

1867
On May 13th the trustees gave Mr Falconer notice to quit. John Bell from Ordley School was offered the position but declined.

1869
Joseph Heslop became schoolmaster on November 6th.

SCHOOLMASTER WANTED.

WANTED, at Whitley Chapel, in Hexham-shire, a SCHOOLMASTER, competent to teach English Grammar, History, Geography, and the Rudi-ments of Mathematics. He must be a Member of the Established Church. The Master will have a good and convenient House, and the Interest of £100 as fixed Stipend. The School being in a Central Situation, and without Competition, affords a good Opportunity for a diligent Teacher. A Knowledge of Psalmody will be a Recommendation. Candidates must appear for Examina-tion at the New School Buildings, at Whitley Chapel, on Thursday the 27th Inst. at Ten o'Clock A.M. The Rev. WM. SISSON, Incumbent of Whitley Chapel, will attend to Enquiries on the subject.
Whitley Chapel, December 3, 1849.

WANTED,

A Schoolmaster and Schoolmistress for Whitley Chapel School, in Hexhamshire,

To be Members of the Established Church, and to enter upon their duties at Martinmas next, or as soon after as conveniently may be.

The Master to be competent to teach the several branches of Education usually taught in good Country Schools, and the Mistress to be able to instruct the Girls in plain and fancy Needlework.

The Stipend consists of £20 per Annum, from Subscriptions and Endowment, together with an excellent House and Garden, and Quarter-pence. The School is under Government Inspection.

Candidates are requested to attend at Whitley Chapel, on Thursday the 22nd Instant, at 1 o'Clock, p. m., when the Trustees will enquire into their respective merits, and endeavour to make the appointments.

Enquiries will be answered in the mean time by the REV. WM. SISSON, Slaley, Hexham.

Whitley Chapel, October 9th, 1857.

Edward Pruddah, Printer, Market Place, Hexham.

plate 19

WANTED, a SCHOOLMASTER and SCHOOL-MISTRESS for WHITLEY CHAPEL SCHOOL, in Hexhamshire. To be members of the Established Church, and to enter upon their duties at Martinmas next, or as soon after as can be arranged.
The stipend consists of £20 per annum, from subscriptions and endowment, together with a convenient House and Garden, and Quarter Pence.
The Master may hold the office of Parish Clerk.
Candidates are requested to attend at Whitley Chapel, on *Saturday, the 6th November next*, at One o'clock, p.m., when the Trustees will enquire into their respective merits and make the appointment.
Enquiries will be answered by the Rev. WM. SISSON, Slaley, Hexham.
Whitley Chapel, Oct. 21st, 1869.

Advertisements for the position of schoolmaster / schoolmistress were placed in the Newcastle Chronicle several times during the second half of the 19th century.

SCHOOLMASTER WANTED.—WANTED, at Whitley Chapel, in Hexhamshire, a SCHOOL-MASTER, to commence his Duties on or soon after the 13th May next. He must be a Member of the Established Church, and be competent to teach English Grammar, History, Geography, and the Rudiments of Mathematics. The present Master returned the Income of the above School for the Year ending March, 1851, at £53 from all Sources, including a good Residence and Garden.—Applications, supported by Testimonials as to moral Character and Ability to be made to the Rev. Wm. Sisson, Whitley, Hexham, on or before the 31st Inst. All Letters to be pre-paid.—Whitley Chapel, March 10th, 1852.

Whitley Chapel School   c.1910

plate 20

plate 22

plate 21

William Angus Blackburn lived at Steel Hall all his life. In 1873 he was an 13 year old pupil at Whitley Chapel school when he wrote in this exercise book.

Examples of his work are shown on the next two pages:

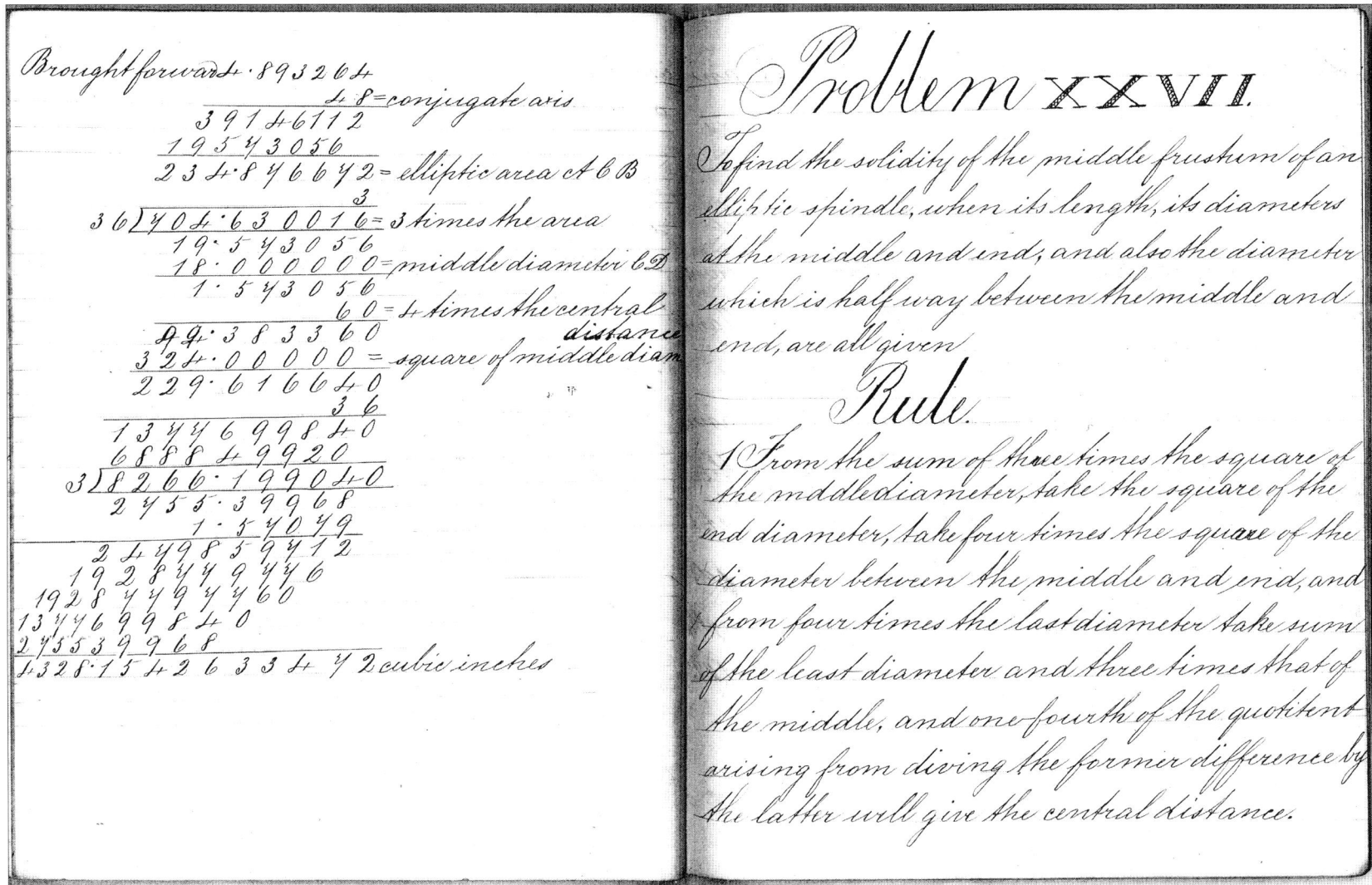

Brought forward · 8 9 3 2 6 4

             4 · 8 = conjugate axis

      3 9 1 4 6 1 1 2

     1 9 5 7 3 0 5 6

    2 3 4 · 8 7 6 6 7 2 = elliptic area A C B

                3

3 6) 7 0 4 · 6 3 0 0 1 6 = 3 times the area

    1 9 · 5 7 3 0 5 6

    1 8 · 0 0 0 0 0 0 = middle diameter C D

     1 · 5 7 3 0 5 6

        6 0 = 4 times the central

                distance

   9 4 · 3 8 3 3 6 0

   3 2 4 · 0 0 0 0 0 = square of middle diam

   2 2 9 · 6 1 6 6 4 0

             3 6

  1 3 7 7 6 9 9 8 4 0

  6 8 8 8 4 9 9 2 0

3) 8 2 6 6 · 1 9 9 0 4 0

   2 7 5 5 · 3 9 9 6 8

     1 · 5 7 0 7 9

   2 7 4 9 8 5 9 7 1 2

  1 9 2 8 7 7 9 7 4 4 6

1 9 2 8 7 7 9 7 7 6 0

1 3 7 7 6 9 9 8 4 0

2 7 5 5 3 9 9 6 8

4 3 2 8 · 1 5 4 2 6 3 3 4 7 2 cubic inches

Problem XXVII.

To find the solidity of the middle frustum of an elliptic spindle, when its length, its diameters at the middle and end, and also the diameter which is half way between the middle and end, are all given

Rule.

1 From the sum of three times the square of the middle diameter, take the square of the end diameter, take four times the square of the diameter between the middle and end, and from four times the last diameter take sum of the least diameter and three times that of the middle, and one fourth of the quotient arising from diving the former difference by the latter will give the central distance.

fig. 1

Pages from William Angus Blackburn's exercise book

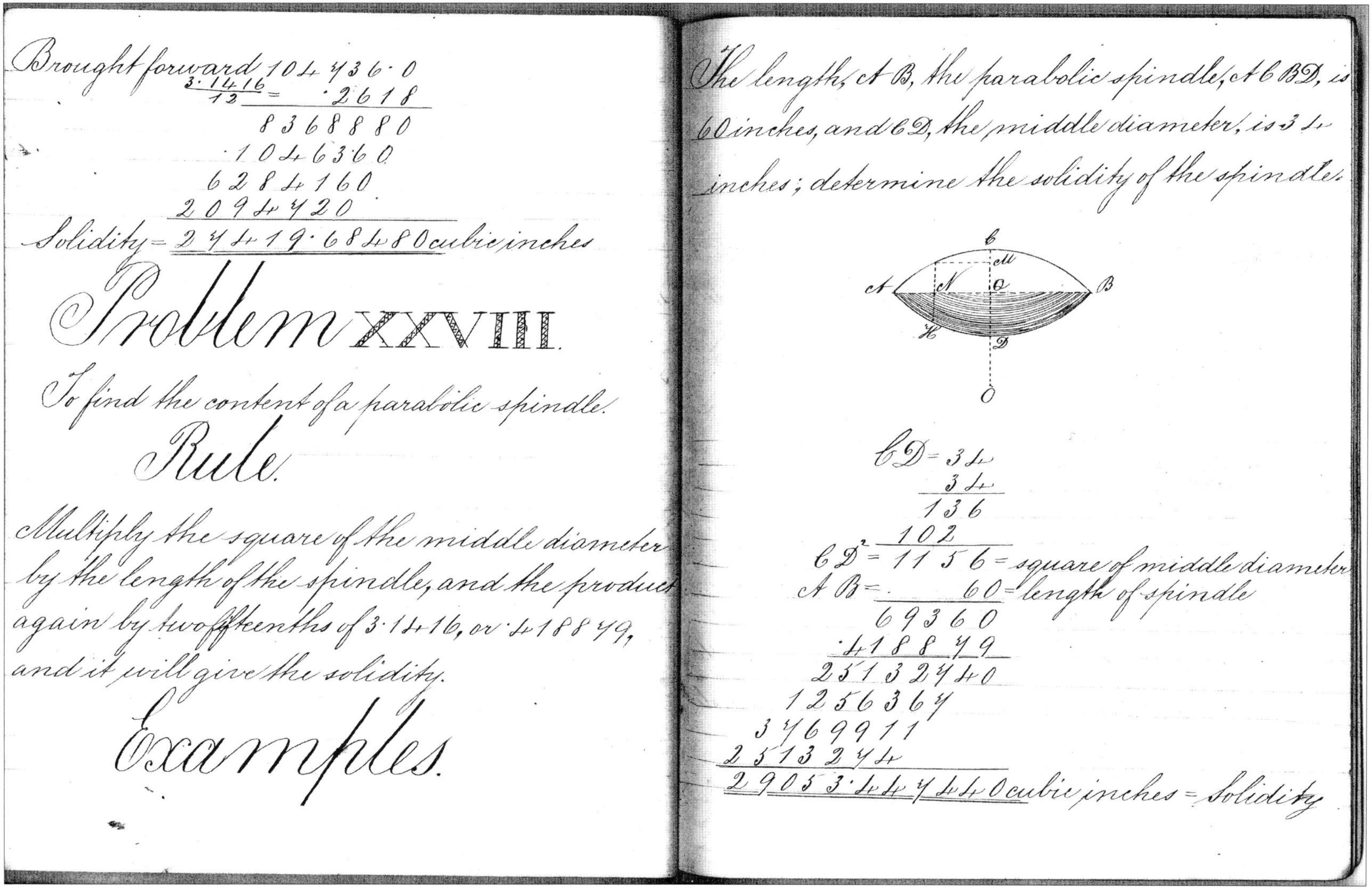

Brought forward 104736·0

$$\frac{3·1416}{15} = ·2618$$

8368880

1046360

6284160

2094720

Solidity = 274 19·68480 cubic inches

Problem XXVIII.

To find the content of a parabolic spindle.

Rule.

Multiply the square of the middle diameter by the length of the spindle, and the product again by two fifteenths of 3·1416, or ·418879, and it will give the solidity.

Examples.

The length, A B, the parabolic spindle, AbBD, is 60 inches, and CD, the middle diameter, is 34 inches; determine the solidity of the spindle.

CD = 34

34

136

102

CD² = 1156 = square of middle diameter

A B = 60 = length of spindle

69360

·418879

25132740

1256367

3769911

2513274

29053·344744·0 cubic inches = Solidity

fig. 2

Pages from William Angus Blackburn's exercise book

1887

June 24th - Minutes of the meeting of the Chairman Rev. William Sisson and the School representatives – '*On the inspection of the school buildings and Master's Residence it was unanimously agreed to do all requisite repairs to roofs, doors, walls and windows.*'
A number of books and a new clock were ordered. Metal railings were to replace the decayed wooden paling in front of the Master's House.

1889

Rates at 2d in the pound in aid of the school funds were collected in May: £19..1..7d was raised.

1894

As there were only 24 pupils it was decided to advertise for a schoolmistress as she could be paid less than a schoolmaster.

1903

The schoolmistress Mrs White was given the '*opportunity to resign*' by the school managers, the reason being that the parents were disappointed with their childrens' progress: several had sent them to other schools. The reduction in the number of pupils meant a fall in funds, and therefore in the teacher's salary.

plate 23

Whitley Chapel School 1923

Left to right, back row: Jane Robson, John Robson, Jimmy Dodd, Jack Turnbull, unknown, Douglas Elliott, Winnie Clark; 2nd back row: Dolly Nixon, unknown, unknown, Sarah Bell, Mary Nixon, Phyllis Hall, May Clark, Emily Hall, unknown, teacher, Miss Hughes; middle row: Annie Nixon, unknown, Dorothy Robson, Diana Pringle?, Molly Dinning, unknown, Annie Hogarth, unknown; 2nd from front row: Willie Turnbull, Maggie Hogarth, Doris Hall, Annie or Minnie Thompson, May Clark, Mona Elliot, Edith Robson, Nancy Dinning, unknown; front row: 3rd from left, George Hall, 4th from right, Joe Nixon,, Harry Flatman, Matty Clark, unknown.

EXTRACTS FROM SCHOOL LOG BOOK

1920

'*January 5th. Miss Hughes is absent, having been granted leave of absence on Monday and Tuesday to visit her fiancé who is returning from Egypt.*

October 18th. The room at 9am was so full of smoke that I was unable to take the children in for lessons. As the room has not cleared, the children have been taken for a long ramble.

December 23rd. At 3pm today a sketch entitled 'Japhet's Christmas Eve' is being played by the children. The parents will be present and a collection made to help the school library.'

plate 24

Whitley Chapel School 1939

Left to right, back row: Miss Dinning, R Dunwoodie, D Tailford, E Common, N Crowe, J Burn, A Crowe, E Pigg, A Harkness, J R Dodd;
2nd back row: K Elliot, N Tailford, N Common, J Purvis, P Oliver, D Burn, M Myers, J Jewitt, J Common;
2nd from front row: W Bell, J Burn, S Turnbull, A Elliot, D Burn, N Lowdon, B Curry, E Snowdon, N Turnbull, R Reed;
Front row: P Dobson, R Curry, A Crowe, A Burn, T Burn, ?, J Myers, A Reed, G Tailford, T Common.

LILSWOOD SCHOOL

The first known school in the Lilswood area was built in the 1760s near to Hackford but there are no remains to show where it stood. The new Lilswood School was opened in 1830 to accommodate up to 50 children from the High Quarter of Hexhamshire. Due to the exposed and remote location of the catchment area, bad weather often caused attendance problems. This small stone building offered schooling for over 100 years but when it was considered too small, a new wooden building was erected on the other side of the road, nearer to Broadwell House. Due to the low number of pupils attending, Lilswood School closed in 1958.

September the 28th 1762

To the Revrd Trustees of Late Lord Crew

Humbly sheweth that we John Johnson of Whitehall in the High quarter of Hexhamshire and John Ward of Burn Sheild haugh in the parish of Blanchland hath undertaken to Build a School house by Subscription of all Charitable and well deposd persons especially to those who are well wishers to a liberal Education We the Inhabitants of the High quarter living at a Considerable Distance from the Town of Hexham and having no school master among us to Instruct our Children nor any place suitable or Convenient for a School master to live in by Reason whereof we are put to a Great Trouble and Expense in sending our children from home for their Education and some of us whose Circumstances will not admit of sending them abroad are Totally Illeterate. The School House which we design to Build by moderate Compulation will amount at or about Thirty pounds of which we have got fifteen subscribed Therefore we most Humbly Implore your Charitable Benevolence of the said sum and we in duty bound shall ever pray. Jno. Johnson   Jno. Ward

EXTRACTS FROM SCHOOL LOG BOOKS

May 24th 1877 to December 22nd 1916

[Inside the front cover, the school dimensions are recorded: length 21ft, breadth 15ft & height 9ft.]

1877
'*May 24th. Punished two boys for using bad language.*

June 6th. Put up some pictures in school with which the little ones are much delighted.'

Teacher Mr. D. C. Rebecca from Aberdeen resigned March 29th.

1887
A new Master, Mr Robert Bell, started in August:
'*August 30th. I commenced duties, at Lillswood School this morning, with an attendance of 8. Standard II have comparatively no idea of tables. Order is very good. Writing very poor.*

September 13th. Miss Isabella Patterson took charge of sewing &c. this afternoon for the first time.

October 18th. Having suffered much from toothache, I gave the children a Holiday to-day, that I might go to Hexham to have the tooth extracted.

November 7th. School closed. No children on account of the weather.

1888
June 15th. A fairly satisfactory weeks work,

dictation and Arithmetic - very very weak especially Dictation.

June 18th. Sorry to state that Thomas Potts, Adam Potts, and Elizabeth Potts of Heathery Burn have left this school for Blanchland School today, the reason being – the school fees are less. They the children were most decidedly, the most intellectual children in the school and I regret their removal exceedingly.

August 13th. Only two children present. People are exceedingly busy with the Hay.'

1893
'*June 27th. Mary Johnson wantonly broke her Ruler in school.*'

July 15th - Inspector's Report:
"*The children read pretty well, but they shew little proficiency in subjects other than reading. With a good deal of hesitation, and only in consideration of the change of teachers, as well as of the nature of the district, and the staff is reported to be efficient. One of the seats in each of the Closets ought to be closed up. Some of the scholars stoop unduly over their writing. Drawing has not been taught in the school. But endeavours should be made to teach it in the future.*"

I. R. Tomlin, James R. Turnbull
1901
'*January 11th. Attendance very bad. Most of children ill. About 4 inches of snow.*

January 18th. Still very bad attendance. Children suffering from Whooping Cough.

January 23rd. Received information of the death of Her Majesty, Queen Victoria.

February 1ˢᵗ. School closed – snow very deep.'

1902
'March 20ᵗʰ. Attendance Officer visited school – 18 present.'

Planned syllabus for year ending March 31ˢᵗ 1903

'Recitations - "Which Loved Best", "The Pet Lamb" and "The English Boy";
Objects - Stds. I, II & III – Sheep, Cow, Horse, Whale, Monkey, Dog, Rabbit, Hare & Goat. Stds. IV, V, VI & VII – Bear, Bison, Elephant, Camel, Alligator, Sugar, Tea, Coffee, Wheat, Flour, Oil-cake, Hay, Gold, Silver, Lead, Iron, Cotton & Linen.
History - 1688 to present time.'

1903
'March 30ᵗʰ. Two children arrived this morning from Heathery Burn. They have not been since December 1902.'

1906
Inspector's Report: *"The condition of this remote little school remains the same in all respects as last year. The Master who is on the point of retirement has worked hard and taught the children conscientiously for several years, if mechanically, judged by modern standards. The children work fairly well when left to themselves, but they are inclined to whisper far too much."*

1907
'August 24ᵗʰ. A very bad week for Attendance. Hay-harvest still not finished. Weather very bad, rain nearly every day.

August 31ˢᵗ. A fine week.
Hay Harvest approaching completion.

September 21ˢᵗ. Many children absent attending Corn-mill Cattle Show – only 13 present.'
[Corn Mill Show was held at Sparty Lea]

1908
'May 16ᵗʰ. A poor week for attendance. Hexham Hirings brings brothers & sisters home. Five children have left the neighbourhood.'

1916
'March 27ᵗʰ. No roadways in snow. I sank twice on my way to school. Only three children able to come.

March 31ˢᵗ. Crawling on my hands and knees in some parts on my way to school this morning. Arrived 8.45, no children present. Stayed until 11.40 doing writing etc. Desks have been changed as the light came from the wrong direction. Am quite ill with intense cold, and no doctor or chemist within ten miles.

July 22ⁿᵈ. I have now been here 4 months, and although there is an improvement all round, there is nothing yet to show, as the children are still far below average.
They are obedient, but seem half asleep. The mental arithmetic, which is still very bad, was nil. Multiple Tables were not known, but are now mastered by the upper division to end of 13ᵗʰ line, & by lower division to 6ᵗʰ line. In lower division girls, money value is not understood. Writing is bad, but improving, spelling bad & deplorable in lower division. Reading very bad, and the 4 top girls who can read, do so in a monotonous metalic voice, with a peculiar gutteral sound to the 'r', & 'i' is sounded like 'o'. Children could not answer any History or Geography. The school has been closed for want of a teacher for 3 months before I came, and had been managed by

the wife of the last master for 6 months.

September 20ᵗʰ. The children have been working very hard at their lessons these last two weeks, & a great improvement is shown all round in everything. At the last examination in reading there was a great improvement. The monotonous sing song style has disappeared, especially amongst the girls, not only in their reading but also in their recitation.

Sepember 25ᵗʰ. Only 8 present this morning. Some of the children gathering peat.

December 15ᵗʰ. I intend resigning my situation at Lilswood School as I find it impossible to stay, being charged 21 shillings per week for board. There are twelve scholars on the Register.

December 22ⁿᵈ. This is my last day in Lilswood School. I have had to pay my own expenses and 21/- for board and lodgings. I have been a teacher for twenty years but have only now found out how badly a teacher can be treated.'

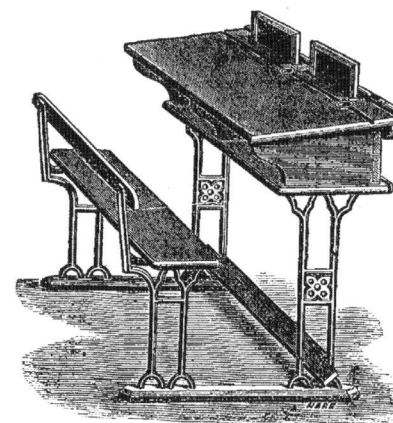

Right - Lilwood school, built in 1830.

Below - Photo of the teacher and her pupils standing outside their new wooden school building.

plate 26

plate 25

LILSWOOD SCHOOL 1946

Left to right: Teacher at back, Mrs Jobson;
Back row: Norman Longstaffe from Steel Grove; Ivan Hull from Whitehall; Margaret Mason from Litharge; Billy Murphy from Riddlehamhope; Patricia Mole from Lilswood Chapel; Edna Mason from Litharge; Roger Dobson from Hesleywell; Catherine Cooper from Litharge Lodge.
Front row: Brian Hull from Whitehall; George Dobson from Hesleywell; Margaret Johnson from Harwood Shield; Edith Patrick from Newbigginhope.

plate 27

LILSWOOD SCHOOL 1933

Left to right: Jimmy Longstaff, Jimmy Common, Ida Patrick, Nancy Common, Jonathon Lee, Miriam Couper, Ted Heslop, Margaret Lee, Bill Kennedy, Annie Longstaff, ? Grieve, George Hastings, Billy Kennedy (Burnshieldhaugh), David Flatman, Peggy Grieve, Albert Common, Bert Flatman.

ORDLEY SCHOOL

The 19th century school at Ordley provided education for the children from the Low Quarter and surrounding area until its closure in December 1948.

School Treat

On Friday the 5th the children attending Ordley School were, according to annual custom, supplied with tea and fruit cake by Capt. Atkinson and the Misses Atkinson of Newbiggin. Each child also received a bun, orange, cracker, and picture book. Owing to the the severity of the weather, many were unable to be present, but supplies of the cake, buns &c. were sent to each of the absentees.

Hexham Courant January 13th 1894

Ordley School, Hexhamshire

plate 28

EXTRACTS FROM SCHOOL LOG BOOK
1918 to 1927

1918
'*November 18th. Several children absent with bad colds. The parents are afraid of them catching influenza so prevalent in Hexham.*'
[3-5% of the world's population died in this pandemic, so parents' worries were justified.]
'*December 18th. Further closure for influenza as no-one turned up for school, then received word from the Medical Authority to close until January 6th 1919.*'

1923
July 3rd. Inspector's Report:
"*The scheme of work is suitable and is now prepared in detail. This school continues to be well taught. In the more important subjects the children are very well advanced and take a lively interest in their work. An effort should be made to cultivate a better tone in singing.*"

1925
'*September 23rd. No less than 11 children are absent this afternoon, visiting a 'circus' in Hexham. This number in such a small school will materially affect the percentage for the whole week.*'

1926
'*May 13th. Closed for two days for Hexham Hiring. Received a picture today from the Local Education Authority for good attendance. It is called 'The Building of the Roman Wall'.*'

1927
'*August 31st. This is my last day for teaching in the Ordley School after 32 years' service. R Parnaby.*'

plate 29

ORDLEY SCHOOL c.1900
Mr Parnaby the Headmaster on left

ORDLEY SCHOOL 1933

plate 30

Back row: Miss Henderson, Johnnie Nichol, Sidney Davison, Alan Simpson, Anty Charlton, Robbie Steel, Ridley Roddam, Robert Dodd, Miss Brown.
2nd back row: Ivy Turnbull, Joyce Simpson, Joan Robson, Violet Watson, Irene Davison, Phyliss Appleby, Dorothy Foster.
2nd front row: Ivy Swallow, Sheila Davison, Edith Jewitt, Kitty Turnbull, Doreen Simpson, Sadie Turnbull, Joan Heslop.
Front Row: Bily Nichol, Derek Swallow, Alan Swallow, Frankie Charlton, Alfie Steel, John Dinning, Teddy Heslop, John Foster, Reggie Robson.

plate 31

ORDLEY SCHOOL 1939

The Halliwell Picnic

Picnics were held by various organisations throughout the later part of the 19th century and into the 1920s. The flat 'haugh' field on the southern banks of the Devil's Water was considered the perfect spot to hold the celebrations. The proximity of the Halliwell Spa Well in the beautiful countryside of Hexhamshire was ideal for the picnics.

The Halliwell footbridge was used by visitors crossing from Low Staples farm, on the northern side of the stream; the track from Dukesfield Smelt Mill provided access from the Slaley direction.

Sports days were also held in other areas of the 'Shire including Lilswood and Dalton; these were still being held in the 1950s and included fell running.

Below -
The Halliwell Bridge looking towards the west.

Below right -
Dukesfield Smelting Arches

THE AGRICULTURALISTS' FRIEND LODGE of the Independent Order of Oddfellows held a picnic and sports at Halliwell in 1878:

THE AGRICULTURALISTS FRIEND LODGE of the INDEPENDENT ORDER OF ODDFELLOWS will hold their PIC-NIC and SPORTS on Saturday, July 13, 1878 in a field kindly granted for the occasion by Mr White, Low Staples, near HALLIWELL SPA and the time honoured stream called the Devil's Water.

The Members of the above-named Lodge will march from Woodside Inn to the ground at Two o'Clock p.m. headed by The SLALEY BRASS BAND.

TEA will be served in a Spacious Pavilion, to commence at Half-past Two o' Clock p.m. Adults, 1s; Children, 6d.

SPORTS – Open to all comers.

Wrestling, Running High Leap and a 120 Yards Handicap Footrace. Also a Flat Race for Men above 40 years of age.

Sports to commence at 7 o'Clock p.m.

Names of the intending competitors for Foot Races to be sent to Mr. J. ROBINSON, Woodside Inn, Hexhamshire.

Entries for the Handicap to close on Friday, 12th inst.

Entry, 6d. each

Hexham Courant   *June 26th 1878*

plate 32

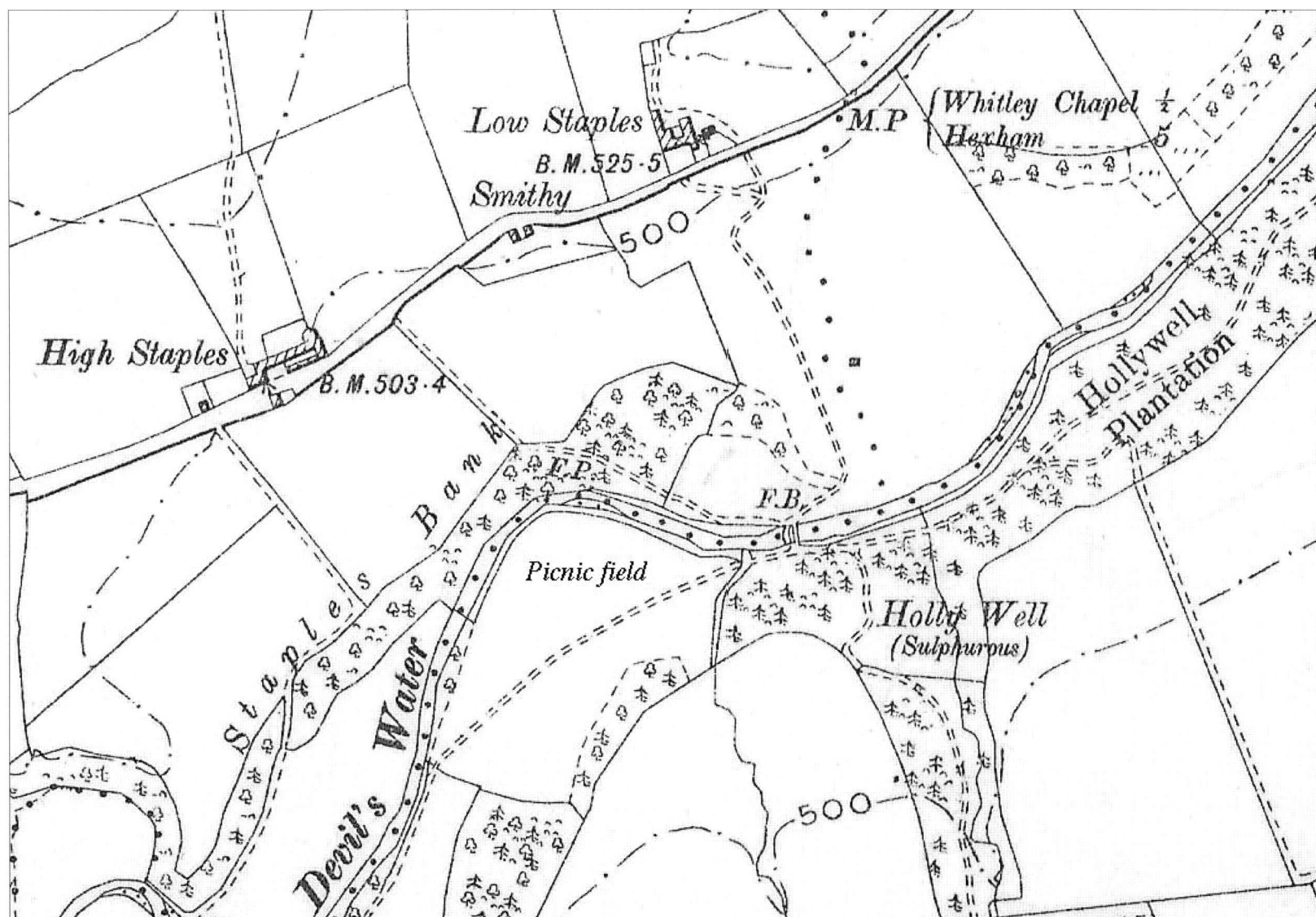

fig. 3

Section of the 2nd Edition OS Map of Hexhamshire 1898 showing picnic field, Halliwell bridge and the Halliwell Spa Well.

The Hexham Courant of July 26th reported that the picnic was a great success, describing the venue thus:

"In lowly dale, fast by a river's side,
With woody hill o'er hill encompassed round,
A most enchanting sweetness doth abide,
It is, I ween, a lovely spot of land."

'At two o'clock the members of the lodge above-named, mustered at their lodge room, at Woodside Inn, and headed by the Slaley Brass Band, under the expert and able leadership of Mr Robert Robson, marched in procession to the appointed rendezvous, when the festive proceedings of the day were at once inaugurated. Tea was served up in a spacious pavilion erected on the ground, during the afternoon, to a very large number of guests, numbering some hundreds.'

After tea the sports began: G. W. Oliver won the '120 yards Handicap Race'; the 'Old Men's Race' was won by John Dinning; J. Burn won the 'Running High Jump'. The wrestling contest, having taken place in twilight, was won by T. Dickinson, Allendale; G. W. Oliver, Dotland, was second; John Ellerington from Juniper was third.
'The above concluded the sports and the company broke up at 10.30, the band, which had kept the fantastic toes going almost incessantly during the afternoon, played them off the ground to "Sweet Home".'

The Hexhamshire and Slaley Friendly Society held their annual picnic at Halliwell in June, one of the earliest of the picnic season. It became known as the *'Halliwell Picnic'* and later the *'Halliwell Picnic and Sports'*.

plate 33

The Woodside Inn, later known as the Clickem Inn or Fox & Hounds

HALLIWELL ANNUAL PIC-NIC & SPORTS

'Linked with the scenic attractions, which are in themselves sufficient to command extensive patronage, - the three essential elements which go to form picturesque scenery, hill, wood and stream, mingling here with remarkable beauty – was the famous Halliwell Spa, whose refreshing mineral waters were much partaken by the visitors. The pleasure if the pic-nicians was further enhanced by the sweet strains discoursed by the band of the F (Allendale) Company of the 1st Battalion Northumberland Fusiliers, which under the able leadership of Mr. Wm. Brown, rendered a varied programme of music during the afternoon and evening, and soon their merry strains the young men and maidens, the latter attired in their charming summer costumes, began to trip the light fantastic on the velvety turf.'

Hexham Courant   *July 17th 1886*

HALLIWELL PIC-NIC

Whether it was the pony racing at Halliwell, or some other participated pleasure, yet there was a number of people much larger than anyone could expect under the circumstances, turned up at the usual trysting place which was in a field near Halliwell Spa, granted by Mr. Joseph Blackburn of High Staples. Among the pleasure seekers were a fair number of the fair sex, who were evidently possessed with good hearts to turn out in such weather, and with "gamps" in hand they trudged through the wet grass, which in many places was over a foot in length, "to see and be seen". The pic-nic is held under the auspices of the Slaley Brass Band, under the leadership of Mr. Nixon, was present and made an effort to relieve the monotony of the day.

The pony racing took place in an adjoining field, and the first handicap race, which was for ponies 13.2 hh secured the following entries:-
W. Maughan, Slaley, (Catcher-em-alive);
J. Robinson, Manor House, (Manor House Lass);
A. Rutherford, Dukershagg, (Jessy);
J. Graham, Dalton, (Peter);
J. Robinson, Manor House, (Snail);
The result of the race was as follows:- Jessy 1st, 15s; Manor House Lass 2nd, 7s 6d; Catch-em-alive 3rd, 2s 6d.
Race about a mile; first won easy, good race between second and third.
The following entries were received for ponies under 14.2 hh: -
J. Hornsby, Park House, (Park House Lad);
H. Davison, Fotherley, (Polo);
R. Richardson (Mosquito);
A. Rutherford (Jessy);

Polo 1st 25s; Jessy 2nd 10s.
Mr. Dodd, the secretary, acted as handicapper, starter and referee. Tea was provided on the field, when Misses M. H. Jewitt, Robson, Bowey, Farbridge and Mrs. Rodham presided over the tables. A ball was held in a marquee in the evening, the music being supplied by the band.

Hexham Courant   June 25th 1892

THE HALLIWELL SPA

Away to the picnic at Halliwell Spa.
The water is pure and best of them 'a;
The tea has a flavour there's naught can excel
When brewed with the water at the Halliwell.

The walks they are neat, the trees evergreen
Bespangle the place with a silvery scene,
The banks they are glooming with flowers so rare
And rivals the garden where nature is there.

The De'ils Water purling its sweet little stream
Awakens the thought like an enchanted dream,
Where trout they are jumping like a magic spell
Refreshed with the stream as it comes from Halliwell.

The Pic Nic again I would wish to report
Where lads and young lasses they often resort,
Where hearts full of love their stories may tell
As they rove on the banks at the Halliwell.

You talk of the grandeur of Starwood Le Peel
Where warriors have fought with the glittering steel,
But to talk of these heroes their deeds for to tell
They still would come short of the old Halliwell.

The 'Holy Well' or Halliwell Spa Well

O could I find language to flow at my will
The old Halliwell I would advocate still,
I would tell of its flowers there's naught can excel
The wonderful cures made by the famed well.

O could I but sound it to the East and the West
Of all the spa waters I am sure it's the best,
The wonderful cures I'm glad for to tell
So many's been made by the old Halliwell.

O could I entreat you to give it a try
When health it is wanting no one can it buy
But when it is wanting and you want a cure
At Halliwell Spa you will find it I'm sure.

This poem was dedicated to Miss Mary Bell of Mollersteads,

August 17th, 1873, writer unknown

The remains of the 'Holy Well' c.1900. The water was reputed to be charged with sulphurated hydrogen. The old pump is still standing but in poor repair; the area is extremely overgrown.

plate 34

HALLIWELL PIC-NIC AND SPORTS

Saturday last added another pic-nic to those in the past, held under the auspices of the Slaley Brass Band, and at the most lovely pic-nic resort known as Halliwell Spa. A field lying to the south side of the Devil's Water, and only about one hundred yards from the famous Spa, was placed at the disposal of the committee by Messrs Blackburn, and in it the various events were brought off.
As might be expected the lovely day was the means of bringing together numbers both from the districts of the Shire and Slaley. To the strains of the band, the lasses, varying from "sweet sixteen" to "fair, fat and forty" tripped the "light fantastic" with their more sturdy swains on the green sward, under the blue canopy of heaven, and with no menacing clouds to raise fears of getting a new dress spoiled. The wants of the "inner man" were amply provided for under the shade of the marquee, and the refreshing cup was largely partaken of.

Hexham Courant   June 23rd 1894

HALLIWELL TEMPERANCE FESTIVAL

The first Temperance picnic organised by the Dyehouse Chapel was held in June 1889; it was to become an annual event with the united camp meeting held on the following day, being Sunday. Children from the Dyehouse Sunday School were treated to tea at the picnic; in 1907 the cost to the chapel was 7s 8d; in 1908, 6s 8d; in 1909, 5s 0d and in 1913, 5s 0d – either fewer children attended or the tea was getting cheaper!
In 1899 there was great concern about whether dancing to the band was appropriate at their picnic:

plate 35

DANCING OR NO DANCING?

On Monday night last, an adjourned meeting was held in the Dyehouse Chapel to consider this question. For the last few years, after the speaking and sports at the festival were over, it has been the custom to have a dance on the green-sward for an hour or so, but at the last meeting held to make arrangements this subject was broached, and this adjourned meeting was the result.

Contrary to the usual custom there was a good attendance and the discussion was both pro-longed and animated; in fact, so much so that the rule, "Not more than three at once, please", would have worked well. Mr. Lambert, Slaley, took the chair, and after reviewing the work al-ready done, he called upon Mr. R. Ridley, to move his motion, which was "That we engage a band to play sacred music only", after moving which he (Mr. Ridley) said it was not creditable to them as Christian Churches to put, as they were doing, a stumbling block in their members' way.

Dancing was to their Church a much greater curse than drink was, and if they (the representa-tives of the Shire Churches) did not find it a curse

plate 36

to them, it was to their Slaley Chapel. They had already lost members by it, and he claimed it was their duty to assist in stamping it out. Mr. C. Robson, Slaley, seconded.

He appealed to the chairman to read the 14th chapter of Romans, which was read as requested – Mr. Simpson, secretary, said that, in his private capacity, he would certainly advocate a policy of non-interference in this matter. He would remind them that Saturday's gathering was not a religious gathering at all, but one to promote temperance principles, and they at Churches, had no responsibilities resting on them.

This Saturday's gathering was distinct from the Sunday's gathering, and the latter had to rely on the charity of the former. The dancing had only

been carried on after the band's engagement with them was up, and they were, for their extra playing, remunerated by a collection among the dancers. He was not a dancer himself, but he thought they ought not to take such a narrow view of the matter. Dancing was not compulsory but he would say to those who wanted to dance let them dance. His amendment was practically a direct negative to the motion.

After more animated discussion, votes for the amendment 8, and for the motion 5, and one member abstained, 'so that the young men and maidens of the Shire and Slaley will again be able to step the to the strains of the Hexham C. E. T. Band, 'neath the spreading trees at Halliwell.'

Hexham Courant   *June 24th 1899*

HALLIWELL SCHOOLS' PIC-NIC

On Saturday last Whitley, Ordley, and Lilswood school children were entertained to tea in the Halliwell pic-nic field, lent for the afternoon by Mr. W. White, Low Staples. Funds were left in the hands of the Pretoria Celebration Committee last year, and it was decided to spend that, together with some additional subscriptions, kindly collected by Miss Thorburn and Mr. W. Nixon, in providing a pic-nic for the whole of the children of the shire. The Whitley scholars paraded at their school, and were marched to the field by their school mistress, Mrs. White. The Ordley children were under their master, Mr. R. Parnaby, while Mr. G. D. Little looked after the interests of the Lilswood school, in the absence of their teacher. The afternoon was fine, and the outing in the beautiful Halliwell grounds was thoroughly enjoyed by about 120 sturdy lads and lasses, as well as a good number of the general public. A programme of sports, in which the children showed a keen interest and healthy rivalry, was brought off under the direction of Messrs. Parnaby, W. Nixon, W. Hall, and some good races were witnessed. The interest taken by the various schools in the Tug o war was great and the proud demeanour of the little champions was amusing. The tea tables were well patronized, and the various duties appertaining thereto were discharged by Mrs Neilson, Mrs Charlton and Mrs Scott. A sweet stall under Mr. Jos.Clark and Mr. Newby, South Shields, received much attention. The results of the sports were as follows:-

Foot Race (boys)- Heat 1: 1st W. Walton; 2nd E. Appleby. Heat 2: 1st R. Herdman; 2nd T. Charlton. Heat 3: 1st H. Henderson; 2nd G. E. Scott. Heat 4: 1, J .R. Thompson; 2, J. Charlton. Semi-finals- Heat 1: 1st W. Walton; 2nd E. Appleby. Heat 2: 1st G .E. Scott; 2nd H.Henderson. Final

plate 37

-1st H Henderson; 2nd G.E.Scott; 3rd E.Appleby; 4th W. Walton.

Girls Race – Heat 1: 1st M. Wilkinson; 2nd N. Ridley. Heat 2: 1st E. Dodd; 2nd A. Barron. Final- 1st M. Wilkinson; 2nd A. Barron; 3rd N. Ridley; 4th E. Dodd.

Three-legged Race (boys)- Heat 1: 1st R. Bowman and J. Charlton; 2nd J .R. Thompson and H .G .Simpson. Heat2:(girls): 1st E. Henderson and M. E. Lowdon; 2nd A Barron and N. Ridley. Final: 1st E .Henderson and M. E. Lowdon; 2nd J. R. Thompson and H. G. Simpson; 3rd A. Barron and N. Ridley.

Tug-o-War (boys)-1st Whitley School; 2nd Ordley School; 3rd Lilswood School.

Tug-o-War (girls)-1st Whitley; 2nd Ordley.

Jockey Race- 1st T .Charlton and J. Bowman; 2nd J. Henderson and J. W. Carr; 3rd E. Appleby and G. Lowdon; 4th W. Walton and C. Hall.

During the afternoon music was supplied by the Hexham C.E.T.S Band, under the leadership of Mr. M. Snowball. At night the adults had their turn, and a well attended ball was held in a large marquee, the M.C. being Mr. Parnaby and Mr. J. Blackburn. The Committee thankfully acknowledge receipt of subscriptions from the following:- Messrs. W. Wear, J. Blackburn, J. Johnson, E. S. Lee, J .Robson, W. Ridley, A. Heslop, J. Henderson, J. Nixon, T. Simpson, W. Hutchinson, Misses Nichol and Errington, and Mrs. Dawson. During the afternoon, among other people, we noticed the veteran Vicar of Slaley, the Rev.W. Sisson, together with his two daughters.

Hexham Courant   *June 1901*

HALLIWELL SPORTS

AND

AGRICULTURAL SHOW

Catalogue of Entries

At the SHOW to be held in the

School Fields, Whitley Chapel

(Kindly lent by Mrs. APPLEBY),

On Saturday, August 12th, 1922.

Price - SIXPENCE.

H. ROBSON & SONS PRINTERS HEXHAM

plate 38

Catalogue of Entries

CATTLE.

Class 1.

For the Best Dairy Cow in Calf or in Milk (the prize
to be withheld till the winners prove in calf, if
not giving milk at the time) (Open) ... £1 0 0
Second 0 10 0
Third 0 5 0

1 Mr G. W. Milburn, Lilswood, "Daisy," sire, "Wedding Gift"
2 Mr Carr, Loaning, "Mary," roan
3 Mrs Salisbury, Slaley, "Princess Etta," light roan
4 Mr Foster, Barker House, roan
5 Mr Common, Park House, roan
6 Mr Maughan, Slaley, "Jane," red and white
7 Mr F. W. Pratt, High Eshells, "Dainty," roan
8   Do   do   "Phœbe," roan
9 Mr Wm. Ellerington, Juniper
10 Mr R. Wright, Tenter House
11 Mr Bowman, Oakfield, red
12 Mrs Baty, Dipton Mill, "Betty"
13 Mr Bell, Rawgreen

Class 2.

For the Best Dairy Heifer, not more than four
Broad Teeth, in Milk or in Calf (Open)   £1 0 0
Second 0 10 0
Third 0 5 0

1 Mr A. Elliott, Staples, Hexham, roan
2   Do   do   roan
3 Mr Milburn, Lilswood, "Cherry," sire, "Wedding Gift'
4 Mr Appleby, Woodside Inn, "Mary," red and white
5 Mr Johnson, Dotland Park, roan
6 Mrs Salisbury, Slaley, "Princess Etta," light roan
7 Mr Common, Park House, red
8 Mr F. W. Pratt, High Eshells, "Mary," red
9 Mr Wm. Gibson, Sunniside, Hexham
10   „ Dinning, East Wood Foot, Slaley, roan

Class 34.

For the Best Two Mule Ewes (Unfed.) Open   £0 10 0
Second 0 5 0

1   Mr Robson, Townhead
2   „ Dinning, Mollersteads
3   „ Armstrong, Dotland
4   Do   do

Class 35.

For the Best Two Mule Gimmer Lambs
(Unfed.) Open £0 10 0
Second 0 5 0

1   Mr F. W. Pratt, High Eshells
2   Mr Maughan, Lord's Lot
3   Do   do
4   Do   do
5   „ Little, Harewood Shield
6   „ James, Nunsbrough
7   „ Johnson, Dotland Park
8   „ Wm. Hutchinson, Long Lea
9   „ Isaac Reed, Edge House
10   „ Woodman, West Wood Foot, Slaley
11   Messrs. Pigg, Rowley Head

Class 36.

For the Best Three Oxford or Suffolk Cross
Lambs (Unfed.) Open £0 10 0
Second 0 5 0

1   Mr Moore, Holmes
2   „ White, Staples
3   „ F. J. Moralee, Edge House, Barrasford
4   „   Do   do   do

A SPECIAL PRIZE of £3 3s. 0d. will be given for the Best
Five Fat Mule Lambs, shown here, then at either Auction
Mart at Hexham, the first Monday following the Show,
for slaughter (Confined.) Prize given by Messrs J. W.
Robson & Sons. Meal Market, Hexham.

1   Mr F. W. Pratt, High Eshells
2   „ Maughan, Lord's Lot
3   „ James, Nunsbrough
4   „ Johnson, Dotland Park
5   „ Woodman, West Wood Foot, Slaley

Class 37.

BEST GROUP.—Black-faced Tup. Ewe, Gimmer,
and Ewe Lamb (Open) £1 0 0
Second 0 10 0

1   Mr Robson, Westburnhope
2   „ Patrick, Grouse House
3   „ F. W. Pratt, High Eshells
4   „ W. Dinning, Spital Shields

Class 38.

Sheep Dog Trial (for dogs which have not won
a first prize £2 0 0
Second 1 0 0
Third 0 10 0

1   Mr H. Storey, Westburnhope
2   „ Herdman, Stobbylea, "Tib"
3   „ Johnson, Ardley, "Toss"
4   Mr W. Robson, Lane House, "Tweed"
5   „ T. Armstrong, Dotland, "Fly"
6   „ Geo. Carr, Lane House, "Laddie"
7   „ Scott, "Toss"
8   Miss Scott, Wall
9   Mr E. Scott, Wall
10   „ Fail, East Wark

Class 39.

For the Best Looking Collie Dog or Bitch on the Field £0 10 0

1   Mr J. L. Forster, Carrshield, Whitfield
2   „ Robson, Lane House, "Clyde"
3   „ James, Nunsbrough
4   „ J. Carr, Loaning, black and white, "Meg"
5   „ Appleby, Woodside Inn, "Teddie"
6   „ Geo. Thain, Beaufront Wood Head
7   „ Isaac Reed, Edge House, "Lassie"
8   Mrs Liddle, Smelting Syke
9   Mr R. Davidson, Lea Grange, "Floss"
10   „ Baty, Dipton Mill, "Tip"
11   Master J. Henderson, Hamburn Hall, Hexhamshire
12   Miss Bell, Nubbock

Industrial Section.

Confined to Hexhamshire and Slaley Parishes.

Class 1.

| For the Best White Loaf ... ... | £0 | 10 | 0 |
| Second ... ... | 0 | 5 | 0 |

1 Mrs Lowdon, Moss House
2 „ Dawson, Juniper
3 „ Purvis, Dukesfield Mill
4 Miss Oliver, Slaley
5 „ Phillipson, Earthy Mires
6 „ Wilson, Traveller's Rest
7 „ Crow, Low House, Slaley
8 Mrs Hall, Moss Close
9 „ Brown, Hagwood
10 „ Dart, Lightside
11 Miss Forster, Finechambers
12 Mrs Ellerington, Juniper
13 „ Bowman, Blackhall Mill
14 „ Simpson, Dye House
15 „ Teasdale, Do
16 „ Charlton, Do
17 Miss Henderson, The Lea
18 Mrs Hamilton, Juniper
19 „ Hogarth, Steel
20 „ Johnson, Ardley
21 „ Moore, Holmes
22 „ Batey, Dipton Mill

Class 2.

| For the Best Brown Loaf ... ... | £0 | 10 | 0 |
| Second ... ... | 0 | 5 | 0 |

1 Miss A. Patrick, Grouse House
2 Mrs Clark, Rennies Barn
3 Miss Crow, Low House
4 Mrs Brown, Hagwood
5 Miss Forster, Finechambers
6 Mrs Ellerington, Juniper
7 „ Rodham, Dye House
8 „ Teasdale, Do
9 „ Robson, Lane House
10 „ Johnson, Ardley

Class 3.

| For the Best Teacakes (Currants) ... ... | £0 | 10 | 0 |
| Second ... ... | 0 | 5 | 0 |

1 Mrs Dawson, Juniper
2 Miss Wilson, Traveller's Rest
3 Mrs Hall, Moss Close
4 „ Brown, Hagwood
5 „ Donison, Lea Grange
6 „ Bowman, Black Hall Mill
7 „ Rodham, Edge House
8 „ Teasdale, Dye House
9 „ W. Charlton, Dye House
10 „ Hamilton, Juniper
11 „ Hogarth, The Steel
12 „ Davison, Black Hall Mill
13 „ Robson, Lane House
14 „ Dart, Lightside

Class 4.

| For the Best Six Girdle Cakes (Plain) ... | £0 | 5 | 0 |
| Second ... ... | 0 | 2 | 6 |

1 Mrs Little, Low Eshells
2 „ Brown, Hagwood
3 „ Davison, Lea Grange
4 „ Simpson, Cocker Letch
5 „ Armstrong, Pasture House
6 „ Reay, Peth Head
7 „ Rodham, Dye House
8 „ Simpson, Do
9 Miss L. Simpson, Juniper
10 Mrs Robson, Lane House
11 „ M. G. Dinning, Spital Shield

Class 5.

| For the Best Six Girdle Cakes ... ... | £0 | 5 | 0 |
| Second ... ... | 0 | 2 | 6 |

1 Mrs Little, Low Eshells
2 „ Brown, Hagwood
3 „ Donison, Lea Grange
4 „ Simpson, Cocker Letch
5 „ Ellerington, Juniper
6 „ Armstrong, Pasture House
7 „ Reay, Peth Head
8 „ Rodham, Dye House

9   Mrs Simpson, Dye House
10 Miss L. Simpson, Juniper
11 Mrs Robson, Lane House
12   „   Johnson, Ardley
13   „   M. G. Dinning, Spital Shield

Class 6.

SPECIAL PRIZE for the Best Two Loaves of Bread, to be made from Messrs A. & G. Little's, Ltd., Paragon Flour, 1st, 10st. Paragon Flour; 2nd, 5st. Paragon Flour.

1   Mrs Nixon, Red Lead Mill
2   „   Lowdon, Moss House
3   „   Dawson, Juniper
4   „   Purvis, Dukesfield Mill
5   Miss Philipson, Earthy Mires
6   „   Wilson, Traveller's Rest
7   „   Crow, Low House, Slaley
8   Mrs Hall, Moss Close
9   „   Brown, Hagwood
10   „   Dart, Lightside
11 Miss Forster, Finechambers
12 Mrs Rodham, Dye House
13   „   Simpson,   Do
14   „   W. Charlton, Do
15   „   Clark, Black Hall Mill
16   „   M. Clark, Steel
17   „   Robson, Lane House
18 Miss T. Appleby, Woodside Inn
19 Mrs Batey, Dipton Mill
20   „   Moore, The Homes

Class 7.

For the Best Six Hen Eggs (White)...   ...   £0 7 6
Second 0 5 0

1   Mrs Flatman, Rawgreen
2   Miss Nichol, Turf House
3   Mrs Purvis, Dukesfield Mill
4   „   Lee, Garden Villa, Slaley
5   Miss Crow, Low House, Slaley
6   Mrs Bell, Stotsfold
7   „   Pigg, Rowley Head
8   „   Hudspith, Salmonfield
9   „   Dinning, Molersteads
10   „   Johnson, The Foggett
11   „   Davison, Lea Grange

12 Mrs Armstrong, Pasture House
13   „   Nichol, Juniper
14 Mr J. Nichol, The Steel
15 Mrs Snowden, The Syke
16 Miss Blackburn, Dukesfield
17   „   E. H. Silk, Spital Shield
18 Mrs M. G. Dinning,   Do

Class 8.

For the Best Six Hen Eggs (Brown)   ...   £0 7 6
Second 0 5 0

1   Mrs Flatman, Rawgreen
2   Miss Nichol, Turf House
3   Mrs Purvis, Dukesfield Mill
4   „   Lee, Garden Villa, Slaley
5   „   Herdman
6   „   Pigg, Rowley Head
7   „   Hudspith, Salmonfield
8   „   Bell, Rawgreen
9   „   Dinning, Molersteads
10   „   Davison, Lea Grange
11   „   Ellerington, Juniper
12   „   Armstrong, Pasture House
13 Mr J. Nichol, The Steel
14 Mrs Johnson, Ardley
15   Do   do
16 Miss Blackburn, Dukesfield
17   „   Cowing, Embly Farm
18   „   Herdman, Dukesfield

Class 9.

For the Best 1lb. Butter (Salted) £0 10 0
Second 0 7 6
Third 0 2 6

1   Mrs Nixon, Red Lead Mill
2   „   Maughan, Slaley
3   „   Lowdon, Moss House
4   „   Flatman, Rawgreen
5   Miss A. Patrick, Grouse House
6   Mrs Milburn, Lilswood
7   Miss Nichol, Turf House
8   Mrs Hall, Newbiggin Hope
9   Miss Oliver, Slaley

Songs, Stories & Poems

FAREWEEL REGALITY

And now it's time to say fareweel
And though I hope that we may meet again
And aal things may be reet again
We've lived and spent the day

Chorus:
So we'll cry fareweel Regality
And cry fareweel the Liberty
To honest friends civility.
To winter's frost and fire;
And there's nowt that I can bid ye
But that peace and love gan with ye
Never mind, wherever call the fates
Away from Hexhamshire

And what is time that flies so fleet
But just a bird that flies on merry wings
And lights us down in Happy Spring
When winter's neet is past.

Chorus:

Aye, but the curlew sings her sang
And winds her sorrows down the Rowley Burn
As drear as winds the hunter's horn

Chorus:

And as I set the mossy stanes
And dee me bits of jobs, and gap the dykes
I hear the whisper doon the sykes
Fareweel they sigh, fareweel.

Chorus:

Dae I remember? dae I dream?
And did we rightly meet on Viewly Side?
For all this and much more beside
Has got me sair beguiled.

Chorus:

But on some golden autumn morn
Or when July is hazing Dipton slopes
By Whitley Mill or Westburnhope
We'll live and spend the day.

Chorus:

Reproduced with kind permission of writer
Terry Conway (written in 1984)

DEVILSWATER

Up the hill and over the hill,
Down the valley by Dipton Mill,
Down the valley to Devilswater
Rode the parson's seventh daughter.

Her heart was light, her eyes were wild –
Seventh child of a seventh child –
Down the valley to Devilswater
Came the parson's black eyed daughter.

Down she rode by the bridle-track,
Down she rode, and never came back –
Never back to the Devilswater
Came the parson's black-eyed daughter.

Up the hill and over the hill,
Down the valley by Dipton Mill,
High and low the parson sought her,
Sought his seventh black-eyed daughter.

He tripped as he trod the bride-track,
A bramble tore his coat of black,
And he stood on the brink of Devilswater
And cursed, and called her the devil's daughter.

Up the hill and over the hill
Rode a black-eyed gipsy Jill,
Down the valley to Devilswater
Rode the devil's black-eyed daughter.

Rode in a yellow caravan,
By the side of a merry black-eyed man;
Down the bank to Devilswater
Rode the devil's merry daughter.

Her heart was light, her eyes were wild,
As kneeling down with her little child,
She christened her bairn in the Devilswater –
The black-eyed brat of the devil's daughter.

Low she laughed – as she hugged it tight,
And it clapped its hand at the golden light
That glanced and danced on the Devilswater –
To think she was once a parson's daughter.

By Wilfrid Wilson Gibson
from " Whin " published 1918

The Dipton Mill Inn   plate 39

HEXHAMSHIRE
(Spelling and grammar as originally written)

To the south of Dotland park, nestles the little cott of Smelting Syke long know as the Inn of that name, there is little here to entrist the curious unles he has had some acquaintance of the quaint little Inn of by-gone day's, for farmers some fifty or sixty years ago used to hold their corn supper at this place. It was also a sort of half way resort of cariar galaway drivers who brought the ore from the countries to the west to the Smelt mill of Dukesfield. There has evedently been a smelting furnace for lead ore at or near the Inn aluded to, as the name indicates, and born out by the fact of emence quantities of half smelted or what is, technicly speaking, called roasted ore, found in the bed of the small rivulet that pases the house. Before going further to the south we may notice the beautifule situated farm on the top of the hill to the north west, there is a rhyme concerning this place and two or three of the surrounding on-steads it begins with

"Dowley Dottland stands on a Hill
Hungry Yaridge looks at it still
Barker House a little below
Maaks in the kirn at Hamburnhall"

the remainder of this short rhyme is unfortinatily lost it is sertainly curious that this is the only piece of local rhym. We are like-wise in ignorance of its author, it is at least eighty years old. The farm of Dotland is said to have been the last in this locality to dispence with the services of the bull in the plow, to cast a look around the farm on stead of Barker House will not take up much time and may prove interesting to the lover of antiquity. There is some very old cotages here, the sagged roof and crumbling

walls bespeck their great ages. The dores to thes humble mansions have once had the advantage of a wood bolt of emence strength and dimensions which slid from holes in the walls against the back of the dores which it spectuly secured from being burst open by violence. The wood work of these buildings is of the most massive and solid description. This property, with a small country residence ajoining was some 80 or 100 acres the property of a Mr Ord, a man remarkable for his eccentricity. There is a story told of a kettle of gold coin having been found among these antique buildings. To the south of Barker House, at the distence of about a mile stands Whitley Church, a building of no very great consequence, altho it is the only building of the kind that the Shire can boast of, it is built in the plainest manner, without any Steeple, and possesses a bell of very indifference tone, to go into the history of this poor edifice, would be to give a sketch into the past of little more than a century, where we find that a small chapel or building of like nature was apropriated by some wandering Quakers who visited these parts, some where about the middle of the Eighteenth century; for divine service. This it seams fired the Church of England party with indignation and jelocisicy, and succeeding in wresting the small edifice from their more meek and holy enimies.

The minister of Slaeley officiated (and continues to do) there every other Sunday which proved effectual to defeat the designs of the Quakers. The Chapel is didicated to St. Helen.

Looking from Whittley Church in a South Westerly direction, can be sean the upper portions of the Shire, the picture is of the wildest and bleakest discreptions, hire on the declivity of a green knool may be seen a loan farm house or a sheep cott, while on either brow, may be traced the ling clad heath, which stretch uninterruptedly for miles over the mountains, which are alive in the summer with grouce. The next object of interest is the Spar well, situated on the south side of Dukesfield burn about a quarter of a mile below Whitley, the water is of surprising quality, and of much repute, by some people who visit the well in summer season, it is a place of great resort in the evenings of spring and summer to the young people of the neighbourhood. Not more than a 'bow shot' from the Spar well stands the Ruins of the old Dukesfield smelt mill, the two arches of the flues and some of the old chimnies, are the only remains of a building, which once employed a great number of the population of the Shire, the ore to be smelted at this mill was brought princepaly from Allendale on the backs of ponies, commonly styled 'carrier galaways', a distinct breed, which was conducted by a larger horse, well trained to the roads. This was called a raker, and behind in single file followed the drove of ponies composed of from ten to twenty or some times thirty, all loaded with a couple of bags weighing 8 stones apiesce. These droves when seen at a distance resemble a band of pack mules such as are to bee seen at the present day in general use in Spain and other countries. The last vestage of these once common packs was broken up in the Autumn of the present year (1879) in Weardale where they had still kept their ground, until the depressed state of the lead traid rendred their services valueless, and they were subsequently sold by auction, without the least hope of the anticent custom being renewed in the mining dales. The next place worthy of notice, is the Dye House a small hamlet situated about a mile to the north of Dukesfield Mill, it stands near the west hope burn or wester burn

altho some has even declared that it is the Devils water, but the fact is this stream does not take the name of Deils or Devils water, until it is joined by the Dukesfield burn somewhere about a mile and a half to the north east of the Dye House. This supposition is principly born out by the fact that there is a local tradition, that the enemy of mankind once had a strawl up the stream that now bears his name to the juncture of the above mentioned burns where from reasons, which were probeably neaver divulged he retraced his steps. But to return to the Dye House, this place as the name imply's possessed a dying establishment som eighty or a hundred years ago, a large field or enclosure near the hamlet is shown as the Bleach green. Tenter Hill & Tenter House are names no doubt derived from this old established traid. A house of respectable dimensions is described as the former posessions and residence of a branch of the family of the Anguses. A short distance up the burn from the Dye House may be seen the vestages of an other ore smelt mill, but which is evidently of much older date than the one at Dukesfield. Vast amounts of slagg lies around the earth works where the walls have been demolished and the stone taken away for building purposes , the timber which grows on these ruins is evidently of eighty or a hundred years growth.

Taking the course of the water, which is alive with trout, and which proves in general a frutifull yeald for the Angler, the reader may emagin he passes two sequestered water mills, on his rout to Nunsbrough which is som few hundred yards below the Junction of Dukesfield burn with that of wester burn. A lover of nature may depend upon finding subjects for his honest emagination to feast upon in this beautifull locality, if he be poetical he may exclaim with natures poets

"our impulse from a vernal wood
May teach you more of man,
Of moral evil and of good,
Than all the Sages can."

The wooded banks rise on either hand to a truly majestic height, is some parts the haugh land's narrow and in others swell out in to the timbred wood forming amphtheatre's of various extents through which the silvrey stream purls in calm and silent grandure. Before directing the attention of the reader to Nunsbrough which may be sighted pearing out of a wooded hill in the centre of the vally just described, we will cast a stray glance at Shield Hall, which is situated little more than a quarter of a mile up the lastren-bank, the subject of this brief notice will be an antient structured of small but massive extent the gables, for it is an oblong structure, is in good state of preservation, but bears unmistakable signs of great antiquity. The centre shafts of the windows or loop holes has been renewed by the present propireotor who is an earnest preserver of such antiquetyes. The enterance is at the east side, the floor of the upper apartment is som two feet thick, flagged above, and arched below, forming a vaulted apartment below of som twenty feet long by twelve or fourteen broad the means of assending from the lower to the higher apartment is by a rude stone staircase built in the wall which is in some parts two yards thick. The dore to this place is wanting, but the show though much worn hinges is still heavily fixed in the stone cheeks by means of lead, there is little history regarding this building, but the judge the age by the style of architecture, and general apearence, it looks not less than four or five hundred years old. Its use as its name would lead us to infir was a retriet for the surrounding inhabitants from the intrutions of the scotch, who on odd ocations mad a raid this far to the south, it stands on an admirable possisin for comanding a view of several miles to the north and west. Retracing our steps to the valley, which we but a short time since left, we commence the examination of Nunsbrough, so named as tradition says from there having once been a nunnery there, it is doubtfull though not improbable, there is not the least vestage to prove that such a building ever existed, there is no sign of architectural remains of any antiquity, the only building on the place is a small farm house, but which is of recent date and erection, the stone no doubt from the bed of the stream below notwithstanding all these grave doubts the old tradition recievs general support. Its odd situation is probiably one of Nunbrough's greatest attraction being perched on a sort of promentary projecting across the valley from the western bank, abstructing as it were the course of the water which winds around in much the same form as an S illustrating the freaks of nature in a high degree, standing on one of the eminences near it it is scarcely possible to emagin a more delightfuller sean; in the valley speeds on at a lazey place the stream which some times cources over a rockey an pebley bed sometimes is hushed to silence, in an eddying pool. In the over haning bank rise the gnarled oak or the towering larch, while here and there apears the silent and modest birch drooping and swaying its tender branches to the brees. In few words it presents a delightfull retriet for boath a naturalist artist and angler.

Pursuing the selvyn cource of the Deals water for near a mile, in a north easterly direction, the stream is again increased by the dipton burn here emptying its-self into it, a short way up this illusterous tributary near the lower turnpike leading to Hexham stand's Newbeggin House

the residence of Capt. Atkinson. It is a very neat building surrounded or partely by a small park, it was once the residence of the queller of the London riot.

Again resuming the cource of the stream who is beautifully wooded and in some parts hemmed in with pricipes where flourish some nice spicies of British fern, a rustic watermill and bridge is next reached, here we are reminded of the poetical words of Rogers

"Mine be a cot beside the Hill;
A bee-hives hum shal sooth my ear;
A willowy brook that turns a mill
With many a fall, shall linger near"

To the antiquary, the bridge may prove the most interesting, in part it tells its own history from the fact that in the centre of the parapet of the present bridge, which is of recent date, is fixed a stone tablet of from 2 to three feet in height by 18in or two feet broad bearing the following inscription. God presve Womfora Erington bilded this Brige of Lime and Stone 1531. In which case there must have been a bridge over this stream in the reign of Henry VIII.

Writer unknown, 1879

THREE MEN OF HEXHAM
A NEW YEAR'S-TIDE VENTURE!

Three men of Hexham did conspire
To take a walk into the 'Shire.

Said they 'To Blanchland let us go
The "Lord Crewe Arms" is there you know'.

The three they came to Dipton Mill
Said one 'I'm in to taste a gill!'

The two they came to "Click-em Inn"
Said one, 'to pass would be a sin'.

The last he came to "Traveller's Rest"
Said he 'no doubt inside is best'.

And neither reached the old "Lord Crewe"
Nor tasted 'Baskers Baston brew'.

The trio yet has not come back
And three good lads the town does lack.

But do not let the good folk think
That these men ruined were by drink.

In country life they found such charms
They're all three wed and taken farms.

They sit at night round ample board
And drive to markct in a Ford.

So lusty cheers give one two three,
A country life's the life for me.

Anon

A SUB-POSTMISTRESS

A Sub-Postmistress stood at the Pearly Gates,
Her face was worn and old,
She stood before the Man of God
For admission to the Fold.

"What have you done?" St. Peter asked
to gain admission here,
"I've been a Sub-Postmistress
for many a long, long year."

The Pearly Gates swung open wide,
St. Peter rang the bell,
"Come in," he said, "And choose your harp.
You've had your share of Hell."

by Nancy Charlton upon retirement from the
Post Office at Juniper in 1998.

Post Mistress Nancy Charlton with Marie Simpson

TALES OF HEXHAMSHIRE

Extract from "Bonnie Blanchland" by G. Carr

My Grannie's friends from all around
Have come to Blanchland Fair,
And at her table I'll be bound
We'll meet some of them there.

Her knitting gear is laid aside,
So is her darning creel;
Her churning must to-morrow bide,
Also her spinning wheel.

She has the house both neat and clean,
Her table richly spread,
While bustling around she's seen,
A cap upon her head.

And as they troop in one by one,
Her face a welcome gives –
She asks them how they're getting on,
Where this and that one lives.

She asks about the many friends
She knew in days gone by;
She messages receives and sends
To places far and nigh.

In winter when the nights were long
We all sat round the fire,
While grannie, with her knitting throng,
Told tales of Hexhamshire.

She told us how she had to work,
Though of it she'd no fear,
How she could use both rake and fork;
How she could bind and shear.

Of what took place when she was young,
While living out at place,
She told us with a ready tongue
And animated face.

Of witches of the olden days,
And fairies of the past, -
Their dreadful deeds and funny ways
Filled us with wonder vast.

She told us of the evil eye
That some folks did possess,
Which brought on all that they came nigh
Sad trouble and distress.

How folks were filled with blank concern
If they came near the door,
For then no butter yields the "kirn"
Though turned for evermore.

And oft she talked of bogles grim,
Most terrible to sight –
How woeful was the case of him
Who met with them at night!

I've sat and listened, as she talked,
With strained and listening ear;
'Twere no surprise if in they'd walked
And said to us, "we're here."

The shadows falling all around
Did but increase my fear;
Ghosts seemed the cause of every sound
That reached the listening ear.

DEVILSWATER

About forty-three years ago (1825) a "constant reader" of The Hexham Courant met a very old man, about ninety years of age [who] gave the following story of the circumstance which led to such a name being given to the water.

In his young days there lived a youth of respectable family. The graceless youth being on a certain occasion mounted on a spirited horse, and approaching a bridge from the west, met a flock of sheep. Instead of waiting quietly until they passed, he urged his horse in amongst them, whereupon the animal reared, and jumped clean over the battlement of the bridge into the river, which was then in a particularly dangerous state from the recent breaking up of the ice.

As the rash and ill-fated rider descended to his death, he was heard to call out, "The devil take all the shepherds," and, as the story goes, the water from that day obtained the name of the 'Devil's Water'.

The ancient man added that he alone witnessed, and testified the truth of the tragic event.

February 29th 1868

'Devil's Water' originates from the Anglo Saxon name for dark water.

A CHRISTMAS SALE OF WORK

December 30TH, 1916

On this particular date at the Dye House was held
A sale of work and a Xmas tree,
And as numerous a company was assembled there,
As anyone could have wished to see.

In the corner was a stall with an assortment of sweets,
Further along fancy work was displayed,
Some most beautiful things both in blending and in hue,
A credit those those who made them.

There was some dairy produce for which prizes were given,
A cake-weight guessing competition too,
And all nicely decorated was the Xmas tree,
A bright festive appearance all through.

And as the buzz and excitement went on all around,
You could hear the ping-ping of a gun,
Then every now and again were the names given out
Who the guessing competitions had won.

There was an excellent supper which all would enjoy,
An appetising and dainty repast,
What more can be said than the gathering was a success,
Satisfactory from first to the last.

DIPTON

Dear old Dipton, how I love you,
Home of all my girlhood days;
Memories of joy and pleasure
Steal around me as I gaze.

On that scene in all its beauty,
With its woods so cool and green,
Where the swiftly running water
Reflects the sun in golden sheen.

Now I see the dear old hayfields,
Where we worked for many a day;
Worked and laughed and chattered gaily,
It was jolly making hay.

Then when winter, cold and dreary,
Came with all its sleet and snow,
Yet there was a charm about you
Fun and frolic still you know.

What cared we for wintry weather,
What cared we if winds did blow?
We were happy all together
Sitting in the firelight's glow.

Now, alas, we all are parted,
Gone for aye those happy days,
Vain regret to wish the past back –
We part and go our separate ways.

Dear old Dipton, how I love you,
Love you now and always will,
Standing so serene and peaceful,
At the bottom of the hill.

by Mrs Emma Moore, Hexhamshire

HEXHAMSHIRE

Once more I have a great desire
To view the Steel, and Hexhamshire
And see again so full of charm
The homely farmstead "Rennys Barn".

The Devils Water full of life
Secluded and away from strife,
Tho' even flowing to the sea
It still remains for you and me.

The fern clad lanes, the golden gorse,
The stream on its erratic course,
And from the stream (a lovely view)
Perhaps I'll get a trout or two.

Wild nuts and brambles there abound,
a quiet spot, there's scarce a sound
The fir trees and the heathered hills
Enthral me, and the memory thrills.

I climb a hill, a lovely spot,
And in the distance see "Lords Lot"
A farm five miles away it stood,
Half sheltered by a wind swept wood.

As fair a sight one never saw,
The working out of nature's law
Could nature, if controlled by man
Be built upon a better plan?

By Thomas Fairless Bell, September 2nd 1928

HEXHAMSHIRE LASS

Hey for the buff and the blue,
Hey for the cap and the feather,
Hey for the bonny lass true,
That lives in Hexhamshire

Through by the Sievey Syke,
And over the moss and the mire,
I'll go to see my lass
Who lives in Hexhamshire

Her father loved her well,
Her mother loved her better,
I love the lass mysel',
But, alas, I cannot get her.

Through by, etc

O, this love, this love,
Of this love I'm weary,
Sleep I can get none,
For thinking on my deary.

Through by, etc

My heart is like to break,
My bosom is on fire,
So well I love the lass,
That lives in Hexhamshire

Through by, etc

Her petticoat is silk,
And plated round with siller,
Her shoes are tied with tape;
She'll wait till I go to her.

Through by, etc

Were I where I would be,
I would be beside her;
But here a while I must be,
Whatever may betide her.

Through by, etc

Hey for the thick and thin,
Hey for the mud and the mire,
And hey for the bonny lass,
That lives in Hexhamshire.

Through by, etc

HEXHAMSHIRE LAD

Dye House

Memories of J Foster Charlton,
Piper and Personality
In a hamlet of only seven houses, the chance of finding two boys of the same age are not very high, but, just over the road in the house built over the mill-race, lived Matt Simpson, the local butcher, and Mr Simpson had two sons, one of whom, Albert, was just about my age. Naturally we became great friends – as they say, as thick as thieves. He once invited me to share in consuming his father's broad beans, and I reciprocated by bringing him into our garden for a raid on the gooseberries. I still can't understand why we weren't sick.

His dad's premises were at Juniper, half a mile up the road, and one day Albert took me there. I doubt that either of us was five years old. He took me into one room, empty but for an iron ring set in the middle of the concrete floor, and persuaded me to collaborate in a kind of ritual. Trustingly, I allowed myself to be tied to the ring by a rope around my neck. Then Albert disappeared from my restricted view, and there was a pause – until Mr Simpson, very, very angry, stormed in, untied me, and warned both of us never to enter that room again.

Poor Albert died of diphtheria when he was only seven. A nurse, charged with regularly removing with a feather the mucous membrane that kept growing across his throat failed to do so.

I must have been about eleven when, out of the blue, my mother asked me whether I'd like to learn to play the piano or the violin. I never even hesitated – it was the violin for me. At once she led me upstairs and, from a cupboard, produced a violin outfit. "Do you remember Mr Hoyle?" she asked. I did. He was our one-time lodger, surveying the countryside for Ordnance Survey maps, and a violinist whose playing had fascinated me. "Well," went on my mother, "when he went away, he bought this to be yours when you were big enough to play it."

So it was arranged that I would go for weekly lessons to my mother's friend, Kitty Appleby, who lived in Hexham.

When I started at the Grammar School there, I was able to go straight from school to my lesson. News that I was learning the fiddle soon reached the ears of Henny (Henry) Pigg, who, with his brother, played for the barn dances in Whitley Chapel parish hall and he called to invite me to "sit in" with them to gain experience. My mother wouldn't hear of this, however. "I know what happens at these dances," she said darkly, "and I know what happens on the way home after them too!" I had no idea what she was talking about.

Our piano was tuned by Mr Tommy Elliott, who lived at Gunnerton. As he also played the violin, it was only natural that he should try out my fiddle. What he really thought of it, hindsight affirms. It was not a good instrument. It bore the usual "Strad" label, and was the sort of thing advertised in the papers as "Suit learner". For a long time I put its harsh tone down to my own inability, and no doubt to some extent this was true. However, to have it and learn with it was to me absolutely wonderful.

My first solo fiddle performance was at the Sunday School Anniversary Concert, and to give me room to play they put me in the pulpit. I am prepared to admit that my playing must have been excruciatingly painful to any musicians present, but my attention was elsewhere. It required iron self-control on my part to go on playing while wave after wave of laughter rippled through the audience. I could not see over the pulpit top and was unaware that a mentally subnormal child had climbed on to the platform below me, and was crawling about on all fours amongst the other children there.

My mother told me proudly that Mr Elliott was also a composer and he had written a tune for the Pipers' Society to be played at Bellingham Show. Now the only pipes I knew then were the Highland variety, which I had heard at a Liberal Party rally in the grounds of Dilston Hall, where incidentally, I saw a white-haired old man speaking from a wooden platform. His name was David Lloyd George. Many years later, when I joined the Northumbrian Pipers' Society, I found in the Society's tune-book two tunes by T. J. Elliott. Then I realised that "my" Mr Elliott's tunes were not written for the Highland pipes, but for the Northumbrian small pipes.

. . . .

John Foster Charlton, 1916 - 1989, was a founder member of the 'High Level Ranters' and a member of the Northumbrian Pipers Society.
He was a prolific composer of tunes in the traditional style, notably 'The Rowley Burn Hornpipe'.

A DIFFERENT PACE

Two horses munching and a skylark tinkling high above in a cloudless sky.

Five o'clock in the morning while slipping a newly sharpened knife into a well-greased finger bar, fitting the connecting rod without getting rapped knuckles, settling onto a sack of hay on the iron seat of the Symms of Newton reaper. Two horse-power gathered up, to take two-and-a-half days to out the twenty acres in front of the house at Rowley Head.

How could you get bored? The pride in cutting out straight sets that you knew the whole of the 'Shire could see from Robson's bus when it stopped at the Litharge gate or the Whitehall Chapel.

The Peeswheeps chicks running before you, their mother screaming above with the odd curlew and scores of seacrows. Two friends to talk to all day, Sandy and Darkie, even if they were only the backsides of the two enormous Shires.

This wonderful pair then shared duties as singletons in the Blackstone turner, the rake, and the wooden sweep. Then they looked on as pikes were built which they then led to the barns and black A. J. MAIN sheds. All for a bucket of oats and an armful of hay.

Was the weather kinder? Were the crops lighter? Perhaps, but this happy team got one hundred-and-twenty acres stored before the eagle eyes of the landlords arrived to shoot on the Glorious Twelfth.

plate 40

I sound a romantic old fool but I know it was better than stinking diesel, flying bits, wizzlers and the like. And how many of you have ever tasted the field teas like Enid Snowdon and Polly Collinson brought out?!

'Roly Burn'
(Edward Robson)

In Grateful Memory

NOTES ABOUT THE NAMES INCLUDED ON THE 2009 PLAQUE WHICH IS IN THE VILLAGE HALL:

WWI

JOHN ATKINSON from Newbiggin - killed in action 29-11-1914.

SURTEES ATKINSON from Newbiggin - M. C. Major (Act) Royal Field Artillery, 2nd son of John Atkinson J.P. Died 7-2-1918 (aged 30).

JAMES THOMAS BOWMAN from Steel, West House - Private, King's Own Yorkshire Light Infantry. Killed in action 28-4-1917 (aged 27).

THOMAS BROWN - 1st / 4th Battalion Northumberland Fusiliers (4/1961) Killed in action 26-4-1915 or 6th Battalion Durham Light Infantry (2658) Killed in action 25-10-1915.

CECIL P. CLARK from Stotsfold Lodge - Private, Machine Gun Corps (Infantry) Son of William and Mary Ann Clark. Killed in action 3-8-1917 (aged 19).

JOSEPH DAVISON from Lea Grange - Private 1st / 4th Battalion Northumberland Fusiliers. Son of John and Margaret Davison. Killed in action 15-9-1916.

JOHN HENDERSON from The Paise - Lance Corporal, 1st Battalion Northumberland Fusiliers. Killed in action 13-12-1917 (aged 22).

GEORGE HOLDEN - Full details unknown but possibilities may be – 4th Battalion Royal Fusiliers (G/16599). Killed in action 13-4-1917/or Durham Light Infantry 101660 / 35599 / 7597 /or Northumberland Fusiliers, York Regiment 9164 3301.

WILLIAM KENNEDY from Eads Bush - Son of William and Agnes (nee Dagg) Kennedy. Killed in action 4-10-1917 at Loos (aged 19)

ROBERT LEATHARD from Dotland Park Farm - Private, 14th Battalion Northumberland Fusiliers. Died 2-10-1918 at Cassel Camp, Germany (aged 26).

DENT OLIVER - Possible details –Private (1523), Northumberland Fusiliers & Army Cyclists Corps. Killed in action 22-11-1917 (aged 23).

JAMES HENRY ROBSON from Lane House - Shoeing Smith Corporal Northumberland Hussars. Killed in action 8-2-1915 (aged 22).

JOSEPH WAKINSHAW SIMPSON from Juniper- Son of Matthew and Margaret Simpson. Private, 3rd Battalion Northumberland Fusiliers. Killed in action 19-3-1917 (aged 22).

HARRY JOHN SPENCER from Hazelhurst (Linnel Dene) - Capt., 9th Battalion Durham Light Infantry. Killed in action 17-11-1916 (aged 42).

WWII

FRED ARMSTRONG from Dye House - Son of Thomas William and Grace Armstrong. Corporal, Reconnaissance Corps. Killed in action 27-5-1942 (aged 23).

JOHN SURTEES ATKINSON from Newbiggin (brother of L & R N Atkinson) - Capt. 3rd Light Infantry Indian Army. Killed in action 1942.

LEONARD ATKINSON from Newbiggin (brother of J S & R N Atkinson) Lieut. M. C. South Wales Borderers. Killed in action 1944.

ROBERT NORMAN ATKINSON from Newbiggin (brother of J S & L Atkinson) - Lieut. H.L.I. and Parachute Regiment. Killed in action 1944.

WALTER ROBSON DAWSON from Rushwood - Lance Corporal, Military Police. Killed in action 10-6-1944 (aged 33).

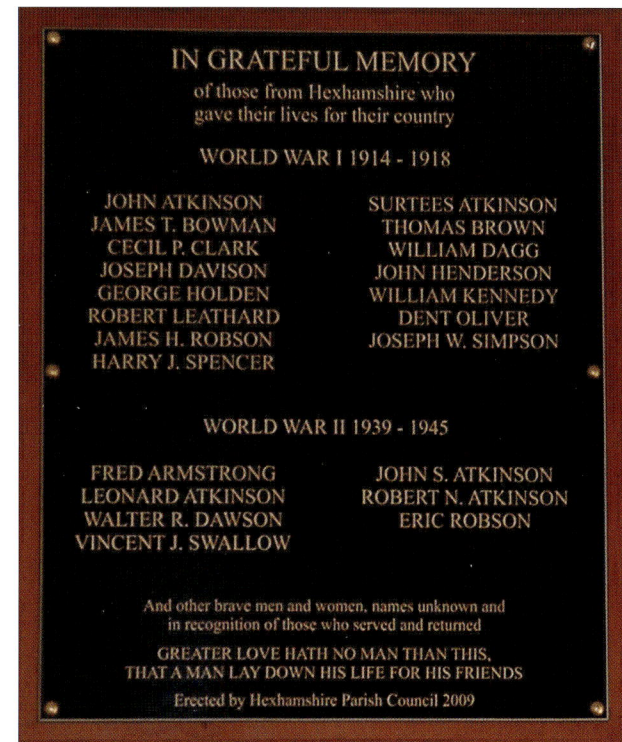

ERIC ROBSON from Barker House - Son of Robert Henry and Winifred Robson. Sergeant, Air Gunner Royal Air Force. Killed in action 4-9-1943 (aged 21).

VINCENT JOSEPH SWALLOW from Newbiggin Hill Farm, Son of William and Annie Swallow. Sergeant, 110 Squadron Royal Air Force. Killed in action 23-6-1940 (aged 23 or 24).

Other names to be included:

ANDREW LITTLE from Oakfield - "Drew", son of Andrew and Sarah Little. 2nd Lieut. 9th Battalion, Durham Light Infantry. Killed in action 25-4-1915 (aged 28).

CHARLES JOHN DARLEY WADDILOVE - Eldest son of Admiral & Mrs Waddilove of Beacon Grange. 2nd/3rd London Field Ambulance, Royal Army Medical Corps. Killed in action in France 3-5-1917 (aged 35).

Pte. James Thomas Bowman

plate 41 James Thomas Bowman and Robert William Bowman

James Thomas Bowman of The Steel, aged 24, and his 22 year old brother Robert William, signed up to serve for 'King & Country' in 1914. Robert joined the Northumberland Fusiliers and James joined the King's Own Yorkshire Light Infantry. James was killed during a battle at Flanders, France, on April 28th 1917; Robert was invalided out of the service on November 10th the same year, returning home having served over 2 years of service.

Letter from James (Jim) to his brother Robert November 26th 1916

My dear brother,
I have at last got a green envelope so I am able to tell you of a little that we have to endure as they are not sensored well in the first place.
Bayonet fitting and physical drill in the morning and learning bomb throwing in the afternoon, and then fall in again at 5 o'clock to go on working party up to the front line until 12, and sometimes 2 o'clock when we get back, as it is generally a good route march from the village and when we get back there are these hard biscuits, I think you know what they are like and of course we arrive back clarts from head to foot and often wet through.
(Jim's letter was sensored after all - a piece of the letter was removed.)

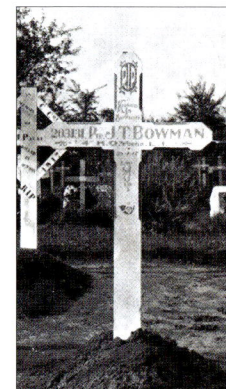

Pte. William Kennedy

26-9-17

Burnshield Haugh
The Steel

My Dear Will

Got your letter on Tuesday date 19th glad to see by it you were well as this leaves us some better. Dad is better except the pains & I am some better hope to be alright soon. I feel very weak. I was sorry to see by your ad that you had been put into a gun section but you never seem to tell us anything. Dad saw Jean at Hexham on Tuesday & she was telling him about them parting you & your mate. I do hope you may get another one you can depend on be very careful my Dear boy & chose a good one with no bad habits as I do fret about you getting led away by bad company but I know you have a lot of good sence. I am sending you a parcel. Dad has taken it to post today he is away to Hexham for coals, look amongst the cocoa. You will find something to buy something with. Fruit – I should think. I will send you some more cocoa next time. I had not much have mixed it with sugar. We can scarcely get sugar.

Now Mary, Bill & family went away on Tuesday. had Auntie & girls from Grouse House last night wanted your new address. going to send you a parcel now I will close hopeing you keep alright. I see by papers it is not so rough at present so love from both and hoping you keep alright. From your loving mother to her dear Will.

Now if there is anything you want to wear socks or any thing just let me know

Mother

William Kennedy, the son of William and Agnes, was killed in action on October 4th 1917 at Loos, aged 19.
There was less than a month between these two letters.

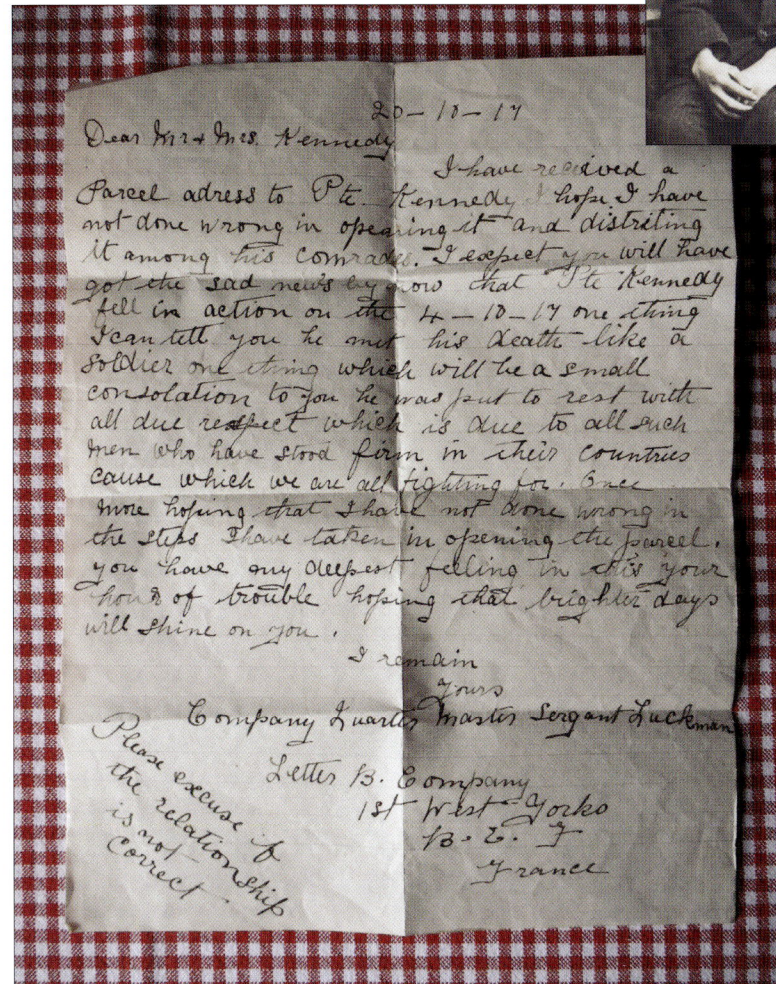

In Living Memory

The following memories were originally published in the *Hexhamshire Magazine*. Sadly some of the writers are no longer with us; their memories are even more important to us now.

· · · ·

Edith Hull Remembers

These are memories of my family in relation to the Shire and nearby parts over more than 80 years.

I am Derek Hull's mother, and was born a Charlton: my Grandfather, Tom Charlton, moved his family from Spittal in Allendale to Earthly Mires, the house opposite Holly Bush at Dalton Chapel, in the 1880's. The Charlton family were living and working in parts of Hexhamshire from the early 1800's. Earthly Mires was demolished in the early 1930's, and stone from it was used to build a byre at Whitley Mill which is now part of Steve Casson's house. Also, stone from Earthly Mires house and outbuildings was used to build a conduit (or "cundy" in local dialect) from the Lightside T junction down the field into the Rowley Burn, and it's still working well to this day.

The Charlton family – my father, grandfather, uncles and great uncles – ran businesses that included a joiner's shop, general builders, cartwrights and undertakers, based in Juniper

from about 1885, and possibly earlier, until my father died in the mid-1930's. One of their inventions was the "Charlton horse cart" built to their own design – quite a number of these were produced, and Ridley Roddam thinks the one at Blackhall is a "Charlton" cart, and that the Pickworth family also owned one.

Some of the Charlton family lived at Dye House and ran a shop there before Ridley's parents. Foster Charlton who lived there in the early 1900's was a great musician and played the Northumbrian pipes in a band called "The Ranters" . My grandmother was a Foster, and they had connections with Foster and Lowe's garage in Hencotes, Hexham, as well as a butcher's shop in Battle Hill. At one time, according to Geoff Brooker's records, there were Fosters living at, and running, the Dipton Mill pub, spanning over 40 years between the 1830's and 1870's.

My mother, May, was a Jackson, originally from Portsmouth, but later living in Leadgate. She met my father, Tom Charlton, when she was working at Tenter House up the hill from the joiner's shop in Juniper in about 1918. Tom and Mary married and I was born in 1921 and we lived in a small cottage at Dye House between Ridley Roddam and Alistair and Sheila Robson. The cottage no longer exists. We then moved to Juniper House – where Kevin Heymann and Trish Sykes now live. I attended Ordley School, and went on to the old grammar school in Hexham, cycling in daily.

When my dad died aged 45, I was 14, and there were a younger sister and two brothers. Obviously money was short, so I left school and went to work at Robbs in Hexham (still cycling in). I also did cleaning and housekeeping for Colonel Robb at Finechambers Mill, and was also employed as a maid at Stotsfold Hall, where I recall that many trees were cut out during World War II to make pit-props. When the Mounsey's owned it, Stotsfold Hall was a fine estate employing visiting gardeners, and included a well-kept lily pond, which is now the Nixons' field pond.

My brother, Anthony Charlton, known in the area is "Anty" and "Uncle Anty" to all his nephews and nieces, was born in 1922, and worked for Harry Simpson (Doris Smith's parents' transport business); he drove a wagon collecting milk from farms, and subsequently became a postman in Hexhamshire for almost 40 years. During World War 2 he drove recovery vehicles in North Africa: when this, on occasion, involved driving through a minefield, he had to master the serious art of backing out along his exact tracks when driving in, and at great risk.

My young brother, Frankie, went into Hedley's "Joinery and Cabinet Makers" in Hexham – and subsequently set up his own shop – picture framers – in Back Street until he retired. During World War II he joined the Navy, but since he never went to sea, he was known as "the dry sailor", and was actually employed in Newcastle to make coffins which were sent out to bring back dead servicemen. My younger sister, Peggy, worked first for Robbs and later for Fells, seed and bulb merchants in Hexham.

My parents and grandparents (who were cart wrights) were also builders, erecting, among others, Finechambers Chapel, St. Luke's Chapel (now a house down Wooley Road), Overdale in High Juniper, and a bungalow beside Kevin Heymann's – once a post office that Nancy Charlton ran, and lives there now. That was the last post office in the Shire.

In my teens, our family moved between Kevin Heymann's house and the bungalow next door several times; they owned both, and as family needs changed moved back and forth.

I've mentioned our Allendale connection; Alan Hull, Derek's dad, came from Allenheads. Derek's great-great-great-grandfather used to run a resting station for pack-horses leading ore from Allenheads to Dukesfield smelting mill. It was a two-tier building – the horses rested below, and the men upstairs. Apart from this connection with lead mining, the Hulls were mainly in farming, and Derek's grandfather, Matt – when he moved from Allendale to Whitehall Farm in the 1930's – drove all his horses, cattle, sheep and hens across the fells to their new home.

Derek's dad, Alan Hull, lived and worked in Whitfield and in the Allendale area, until he met me, and we married and lived first at Kevin Heymann's house in Juniper (where my Dad, Tom, made a recess and built a pull-down bed for the newly-weds in the living room of the family house – the recess is still there to this day) then at a little bungalow at High Staples (by the Macklons' house); Alan worked for Urwins (farmers) and Derek was born in that cottage. In 1951, we moved to Moss House, which was a "starter farm" (this was a Northumberland County Council scheme begun in the 1920's to let out smallholdings to local people and servicemen returning from war to give them a chance to break into farming and there was contention over who got the farms); it was only 21 acres, so the people involved took on extra work to become viable – so Alan also worked out on other farms, dug graves, worked at the mart, and kept "quick return" milk cows, hens and pigs. In 1959 Edith and Alan with Derek (then 10), Melvyn and Gordon moved to Aydonshields and farmed there until retirement.

My father, Tom, ran Charlton Builders, and in 1932 rebuilt the Parish Hall at Whitley Chapel at a cost of £837, having won the contract against a rival bid of £843. (These and all subsequent figures have been rounded down to whole pounds sterling). Tom's accounting books from the period give the following breakdown of the main costs; stonemason £287, joiner £295, halfcaster £22, slater £114, painter £25, spouts £12, heating £43, fireplace £4, closet £2. In 1931 masons and joiners earned £4 a week, labourers £2 to £3, craftsmen were paid 1 shilling per hour.

November 2006

When I Was 10

I was 10 years old when my family moved from the smallholding at Beckside (Low Holmes) to Mire Meadows. My initial memories of the house were of going into a man-made cave. The back door led into a kitchen with a black leaded range at one end and a walk-in larder at the other. The sink had no taps as water has to be brought in from the bottom of the garden where a small pipe ran into the cattle trough. The living room was also dark with its wood beams, dark brown doors and even larger black leaded range. The walls were papered with a dark coffee coloured paper with little flowers on that we could just see with the light from the little window. Upstairs there was one single big bedroom.

The day we moved was busy and quite strange. However we were given a lovely welcome by Aggie Appleby who lived across the road in the Click'em Inn. During the afternoon, while we were settling in furniture, and generally cleaning and tidying, there was a knock at the back door and there was Aggie with a flour bag full of home-made scones and a pot of blackberry jam. "You won't have time to bake today!" That was the beginning of the friendship with her, that was to last beyond the time when she had to give up the pub.

Aggie was kind, but could be to the point at times, such as when we girls were playing on the back lawn with Mum and the bedroom window was shoved open, and Aggie leaned out and shouted "Be quiet you great fond things, Fred's trying to sleep". We all crept back into the house duly chastened.

One of the first things we had to do after we moved in was bring the water supply into the house. After the appropriate consents had been obtained Billy Best was enlisted to dig the trench for the water supply pipes and the sewage pipes as well as the pit for the septic tank. He did the lot by hand.

I enjoyed "being helpful" and was allowed to give Billy a hand with the digging.

Once the pit and trenches had been dug, we had to tunnel beneath the foundations to bring the pipes into the kitchen. I cannot clearly remember most of that task but I do have a very clear memory of squeezing through from the outside and appearing in the kitchen to ask Mum for a cup of tea for Billy and myself to celebrate the digging.

This was the start of over forty years in Mire Meadows. The lovely little house holds so many special memories for me. Thankfully it looks so very different now!

Jenny Evans (nee Capes)

June 2009

Betty Martin recalls

I believe the White family originally came from Allendale, and that in the Eighteenth Century were yeomen farmers, whose menfolk, among other duties, were charged with recruiting soldiers for the King in times of war.

I was born at home at Low Staples Farm in 1935 (my mother then being 45 years old, and my father 60) eight years later than my brother Clarence White. It is part of family lore that father fell asleep during the time of my (or was it my sister's?) birth and came in for some criticism as a result – though it seems to me that he took a very sensible view of his inability to contribute usefully to the event.

My great grandfather, Matthew, farmed Westburnhope from 1850. Once, the house was set on fire as a result of his boiling tar in the open grate – the thatch caught alight. Indeed, he was carried out clutching an old chair, which I still have, visibly blackened by the flames. The family had to move out to Burnt Rigg (demolished now, but then on the hill up from the ford and on the way to Whap Weasel) until the house was repaired and they could move back. Apparently this particular chair was the one on which the bowl was stood in the kitchen for the bread to rise. The ashes in the farmhouse were riddled to see whether any gold sovereigns had survived.
The family then moved to Low Staples in 1865, and in the late 1800s, my aunt was sitting in the kitchen when lightning struck the house. She had a narrow escape, but later a new kitchen had to be built. There were eleven children in the family, two of whom died (Matthew

Henry and John Sidney, aged 14 and 15) from diphtheria. Naturally in a big family, when children left school they were required to find jobs and contribute to the family budget as soon as possible; when two sons reached this stage, great grandma promptly marched them down to the "Courant" office to find jobs. I believe that ponies from the lead mines were stabled at Low Staples, while working at the smelter. In those days, water was carried from the well at the bottom of the hill, and there was no electricity supply until 1951. At the time there was a public footpath there, and even when the builders were adding on the sitting room, an awkward man from time to time insisted on his rights, and would walk across, even climbing through the window! Before my time, Grandma would send someone down to Halliwell Spa (a natural spring in the wood south of the house) for a supply of the health-giving water there – reputedly it tasted absolutely foul.

When I reached school age, I walked daily to Whitley Chapel School, which then consisted of two classrooms – the little room and the big room. There was a black stove for heating, and outdoor loos in the school yard. I ran home for my lunch – not meeting any cars in those days – and my mother would set me so far on the way back. In my father's time there were over 80 children attending the School. We used the School field hill, rolling down from the top in the long grass, often ending up feeling sick at the bottom. There was, to the delight of the children, "sticky jack" in the hedge opposite the School. In those days, the bus from Hexham terminated at the The Black Tree in Juniper, so, if we'd been to the pictures, my father had to meet us. This bus, belonging to Bert Robson, who lived at Smelting Syke.

Of course, this was wartime. My mother and aunt used to attend regular sewing afternoons at the Vicarage for "the war effort", and we came across "enemy" prisoners. One German, who helped on the farm and came from the camp at Featherstone, painted our kitchen; in civilian life he had been a County Court judge – maybe not accustomed to the sort of work we used him for. One of the Italian prisoners made me a ring from a silver sixpence.

When Clarence married Pat in the early fifties, he stayed on at the farm at Low Staples, and my parents, me and my mother's sister, Aunt Molly Richardson (a single lady who lived to be 101), moved out. We used our field at Dye House to build our new home, Deanham. In 1963, I married John Martin, a farmer at Hallington near Corbridge. We returned to Deanham in 1981 and John died in 1988.

I also recall a number of random memories that may be of interest.
Loadman was an "off" farm from which the family gathered clothes' baskets full of lovely mushrooms. In the serious snow of the 1947 winter, Clarence and I made an igloo, and I inadvertently broke all the glass in the cold frame by walking over it; as a result of the hard winter I was off school for weeks, and the icicles in the stable were wonderful. Wool from the farm was sent to Otterburn Mill which turned it into rugs. On threshing days in Summer, more than 10 men had to be fed at the farm three times a day. One of the first hauliers we used was Bobby Herdman from Rawgreen. My father's first car was a Bull-Nosed Morris, and, of course, he learned to drive by trial and error; chains on the wheels in winter were regularly used. I played the organ for the Church Sunday School in Mr Hall's time. At

Christmas when Rev. Lee was vicar we would spend 3 or 4 nights carol singing – dividing the Shire into areas; Pat Pickworth and I swanned around in the dickey of Vickers Curry's car and practised waving like the Queen. We always looked forward to Christmas cake and wine at Stotsfold Hall, where Mrs Bailey the housekeeper held back a cake especially for us – then on to Mary Atkinson's for mince pies – ending up at Walleythorn for more refreshments and to count our takings. The Christmas party was fun – a toss-up whether to dance "The Grand Old Duke of York" with Ralph Curry or Gordon Tailford. Lovely apples were to be had up the house wall, but this entailed climbing out of the granary window and on to the byre roof to pick them – it was who to get there first, but I never fell once.

August 2006

Betty Martin, nee White

My Early Years at the Shirehead by John Graham

In 1932, as a very small boy, I came with my parents to live at Stobby Lea, moving from a cottage in Blanchland village. It was a typical house of that time, only coal fire, no electricity and no running water. This was obtained from a well in the yard. Groceries were delivered monthly by Murrays of Hexham who also brought paraffin for oil lamps and the accumulator for the wireless. E. Carr of Blanchland also delivered groceries and brought corn for poultry feed. It must have been a shock for my mother as she had been used to two grocery shops in Blanchland. Coal was delivered by Bob Herdman of Raw Green.

The sheep stock was taken over from the previous tenant. A few house cows and store cattle were bought at Hexham mart. We also kept a pig and some hens. All farm work was carried out by horse. In the autumn bracken was cut and used as bedding for the cattle. Milk was separated and the cream churned into butter. Skimmed milk was fed to calves.

On Tuesdays the produce was taken to Hexham on Robson's bus which came up on to the Shirehead and around by Hesley Well. The baskets of butter, also rabbits, were carried up a ladder on the back of the bus – eggs went in the bus. Once our basket went missing when the bus reached Hexham. It had been hooked out by a branch near Eads Bush!

There was a good community spirit – when visiting neighbours everyone walked. Whist and dart evenings were held in friends' houses, also groups got together to make rag mats. At pig killing time the goodies were shared with neighbours who gave us some of theirs in return. Sometimes a lamb was also killed.

Whist drives and 'sixpenny hops' were held in Lilswood Chapel, now Lilswood Grange. Sometimes the local vicar, Rev. Pestle, took a service at Lilswood. He travelled in a car with a boot (a dickie) that could be opened to form two extra seats.

When I started school there were about 25 pupils. The only teacher, Mrs Jobson, taught all ages from five to fourteen years. She used to wield the strap to keep order. We all carried our dinners. When walking to school in bad weather I walked close to the stone wall for shelter. When the Patricks came to live at the other Stobby Lea I had Ralph and Ida as companions for the walk to school. Some of the children from further 'out by' lodged with Nicholls at Litharge. Mrs Jobson came out from Hexham by bus but at various times lodged with the Misses Fairlamb at Broadwell.

Soon after starting school I was very ill with peritonitis. I vaguely remember being taken to Hexham in Dr. Stewart's car. How he got the message that I was ill I do not know. After surgery I spent six weeks in Hexham War Memorial Hospital.

My first bike was only for riding downhill – it had a frame and two wheels but no pedals, brakes or tyres! Whatever would the Health and Safety Executive have thought?

My father was Methodist and Sunday was definitely a day of rest except for a small boy who had to walk to Sunday School at Whitehall Chapel. This was run by Nicholls of Litharge. We had an annual outing to Whitley Bay.

The outbreak of war did not affect us very much, we were issued with gas masks which we carried to school and used as weapons to fight one another. We were never short of food having our own milk, butter, eggs and bacon and quite often rabbits supplemented the meat dishes.

When the old school at Lilswood closed, we moved to the wooden school at Broadwell. This has two classrooms so we had an extra teacher. She was called Miss Chilton and rented Steel Grove Cottage. When her fiancé, a trainee vicar, came to visit he smoked a pipe filled with dried ash leaves.

In May 1942 we moved to High Raw Green, but I cycled to Broadwell until the summer holidays and after the holidays began to attend Whitley Chapel School.

March 2007

John Graham

Five to Seventy Nine Years
by Marie Simpson and Nancy Charlton

Two little girls went to school together for the first time in the Spring of 1932 – Marie White and Nancy Crowe. Marie lived at Steel Hall and Nancy at Red Lead Mill.. Marie being brought on a horse through two fields and the Steel Hall wood to Red Lead Mill. There she met Nancy, her brothers and her sisters. Nancy's sister Mary was in charge of taking them to school; a further walk across the Devil's Water Bridge through the Raw Green wood and another field to Moss House. Here it was very wet and muddy and sometimes over the wellie tops (no better today). After leaving Moss House they had to cross the Bog field, which is known now as Quakers Hole. Many orchids used to grow here in the Spring.

The two girls always sat together and managed to get into mischief together. They enjoyed their lessons. As time went on they were allowed into the school garden where they learned about plants, flowers and vegetables, etc. Mr Dodd, the Headmaster, kept hives of bees and also hens. The henhouse was next to the garden. Everyone took turns looking after them – feeding, collecting eggs and keeping the nests clean.

Walking home from school was the best part of their days – looking for wild flowers, pressing them and mounting them ready to be taken to Slaley Show in August. One of the things remembered well was the primrose patch in

the Raw Green Wood. It was the size of a few gardens, a beautiful carpet of yellow!! Marie used to pick them and have them parcelled off to her grandmother in London. Nancy sent hers to a former teacher. Both ladies said the same when they opened the box; they could smell the Shire! This patch is long gone, having been planted with pine trees.

Other things they did was pulling up Pig Nuts which grew in the wood. They picked wood-sorrel leaves, which they ate with bread, left over from the lunch bag; very tasty!

During the war evacuees came to school but very few stayed for long, with the exception of the Dodd family. As time went on the two girls found different ways to get home, by Cobbler Burn or by Mire Meadows, until the Headmaster found out and they had to return to their proper route. School concerts were held, when Bella Turnbull, the hall caretaker, would use curling tongs on their hair. These were heated on an open fire in the supper room.

Sunday School meant walking to Dalton Chapel meeting up with the Commons, Parkers, Hendersons, Lowdons and many more. Time

went on, Nancy's brothers and sisters started school as did Marie's brother Derek. During the summer holidays Nancy stayed with her aunt and uncle in Capheaton, while Marie spent hers in Whitley Bay. Her paternal grandmother would visit them from London.

When the time came to leave school they were both very sorry. Marie stayed at home to help her father, as it was wartime, and Nancy became a tailoress making suits, outfits for gamekeepers, complete with plus-fours, hunting pink outfits for huntsmen and lots more. Later two local boys came home from the war. Nancy married Anty Charlton and Marie married Alan Simpson. Both couples lived at the Juniper. Eventually Nancy managed the Steel Post Office and Marie cooked the dinners at Whitley School for 20 years.

They still live at the Juniper, seeing each other most days, after being friends for 74 years.

December 2006

Marie and Nancy

Doris Smith recalls

My parents, Harry and Polly Simpson, began renting Cocker Letch in 1915 and I was later born there. They bought the house in 1934 for £295 (and it cost an additional £6 for the conveyance fees by Gibsons the solicitors). I married Harry Smith in January 1951, and until November of that year we rented a house at The Lea, then moving on to Black Hall Mill (using Dad's wagons for the removal of course) and our sons Brian and Kevin were brought up there. After that we moved to The Juniper, to the house that Vi and Albert Scott now have, in fact they moved in when we moved out and went back to Cocker Letch in the 1960s. We lived there until recently moving into Hexham.

There used to be a general shop, first at Black Hall Mill, then at Dye House in The Juniper. It was run by Mrs Charlton, but eventually by Ridley and Margery Roddam. The way it was laid out was that when you went in the front door there was a staircase to upstairs straight ahead. On the ground floor there was a door into the shop on the right and a door into the living room on the left. There was a post office in a house at The Steel – the post was brought out from Hexham to the post office, and was then delivered by local postmen on foot or by bicycle.

Beginning in the early 1960s, and for many years, I drove a hire car collecting children for school – at first this was a Dormobile, and later on an estate car. I would go up to Harwood Shield, back to Whitley Chapel to drop children off at the School, then up to Lightside and then along the Drag to Westburnhope. I also went to Dotland and Ardley. My last contract took me to Steel

Hall, returning to Whitley Chapel and on up to Viewley. I once had to stop the bus and tell some unruly girls I wasn't going any further unless they behaved themselves.

There were several schools in the Shire – Whitley Chapel of course, a small school at Lilswood which was moved down to Broadwell, and there was a school at Ordley, which, when children were evacuated from Newcastle into The Shire in the early 1940s, had to work shifts – local pupils in the morning and evacuees in the afternoon. Of course, there were evacuees in all the Shire schools, and I knew one lady who remembers walking from Ardley to Whitley Chapel School – three miles each way. In the winter of 1963 there was so much snow that some children couldn't get to school from Christmas to Easter. I remember Frankie Robson skiing from Westburnhope into Hexham and back during that spell of weather.

There was a butcher's shop in the Juniper, near where Kevin Heymann and Trish Sykes now live. My grandfather was the butcher during and after World War One. Then at some stage it moved to Dene House, and was run by my uncle Matt Simpson. A long time after my grandfather's shop had closed, some new owners moved in and did away with the garden. In the process some bones were found and the police were called because it was thought they could be human remains; however, the less exciting truth was that the bones proved to be of animal and butcher's shop origin, so no national headlines.

June 2006

Alice Margaret Robson, 90 years young

I first met Edward Robson in 1935. I lived on Leazes Crescent with my mother and sister; he lived with his father, stepmother, two sisters – Sissie and Anne – and brothers Howey and Frank, above the west end shop Mr Robson had built at Burncliffe. Edward worked there with his father in the butchery business at Burncliffe and 3, Cattle Market with his sister Sissie. Howey worked as an accountant at Iveson's, opposite the Monument, while helping Mr Robson with farms in the Shire – Westburnhope, Cockershield and Rowley Head, later also at Gairshield.

Workers at the time included George Carr, Jack Goodfellow, Joe Slea, Jack Dodds and Bill Turner at the farms. Edward had lived at Cockershield with George Carr before being needed in the shop. Jack and Joe Collinson worked Rowley Head. Part of the tenancy agreement for Westburnhope meant Mr Robson had to live for six months at the farm, which meant travelling daily to the shops. At this part of the year, the family travelled out on Sundays to have lunch with Mr and Mrs Robson.

Mr Robson snr. was borne at Stone Hall, Allendale. Mrs Robson, mother of Howey, Sissie, Ann and Edward was born Dorothy Martin at Stone Stile, Allendale and died sadly at Burncliffe when Edward was at Barnard Castle School. Mr Robson snr. remarried Winifried Liddle, a widow with two sons, Jack and Ben, farming a smallholding at the time. They had a son, Frank, who, after school at Giggleswick, and the death of Mr Robson, managed Westburnhope

and Cockershield with his mother until his marriage to Mary Vickers, when his mother retired to Osmotherly. Frank later gave up Westburnhope and farmed on his own account at Howick Farm, Kirkwhelpington, until he retired to live at Carlisle near his only daughter, Pamela.

Back to 1935. Edward and I rarely went to Westburnhope for lunch as I found it extremely boring. Mr and Mrs Robson were staunch Methodists, so we were not allowed to play cards and were expected to snooze before tea; Edward and I preferred to walk in the Big Lot! Another excuse was that Edward had bought his first car, a baby Austin, which he stripped down and repaired while I refurbished the inside. When it was completed, Edward took me to Edinburgh and back in a day, which was quite an achievement then.

Mr Robson snr. died in 1937 and Edward and I were allowed to marry – if we had a quiet wedding! I wore a Fenwicks made-to-measure suit which cost ten and a half guineas, and my aunts at Blackhouse, Mrs Hill and Mrs Ballard, gave me a fox fur to go with it.

During the war, we saw very little of each other owing to Edward's commitments at the shops, helping at the farms at weekends, and duty with the Home Guard. Any spare time was spent "digging for victory" as it was called – growing vegetables, fruit and eggs from a dozen backyard hens. However, we did manage to find time to produce three children – Edward, Elizabeth and Ann. The family moved to Summerodds in the 1950s.

Edward married Hilary Alexander in the 1963 storm, and they lived at Gairshield until Hilary tragically died after only a year together. He travelled from Hexham for a couple of years, and worked Rowley Head with George Mason. Edward married Edna Gray from Alnwick and moved to Rowley Head, which he farmed for another twenty years, latterly in partnership with Peter and Jessie Brydon, while managing the shops after Edward snr's illness.

Since Edward's death I have busied myself with Lowgate W.I., Hexham Conservatives, Hexham Flower Club and arranging flowers in the Abbey, pottery restoration, and now carry on my romance with Hexhamshire – playing bridge with friends from Harwood Shield, Stotsfold and Channel Well, and enjoying Janet Brooker's lunches at the Dipton Mill.

2006

Freda Harker (nee Pallan) remembers

My grandfather was the brother of Miss Nichol who farmed Turf House with (in my childhood) her son Norman. My father worked at Turf House in his very early 20s and of course met my mother there. I must have spent every school holiday (and many "flitting" weeks) up in the Shire until my grandfather died about 1945/46. He was a lay preacher for the Chapel and I have memories of the visiting preachers having tea with us (every fortnight, I think). Then off to Chapel. I also remember cleaning Whitehall Chapel – brushing and polishing with my aunt Ruth.

Old Mr and Mrs Bell lived about opposite but don't seem to find any of your photos as being their house. Sixty years on and a lilac in bloom still takes me back to Mrs Bell's garden! The Coopers lived about there too. I think Mr Cooper was the roadman? Also must mention "Fred – the Post", twice a week, on foot, in all weathers. Had morning tea at Litharge and I don't remember any other postman so he must have done that round for quite a few years. Remember going to Stotsfold Hall – think I played with maybe a gardener's children and then the soldiers, including the Aussies, who all had local farms who became "their" places and the tins of meat/fruit/choc. that came with them for supper.

I remember the evacuees also, two of whom spent the entire war years with my grandparents, arriving just after war was declared, from Sunderland. We could roam the fields all day in summer and eat whatever we could find that we thought may be edible.

Life was hard for these Shire people as you well know. Water carried from the "well" – a stone trough where the stream came down off the fells and cattle and sheep used it further up. Drinking water "settled" for a couple of days and the rest filled the boiler by the fireside.

March 2006

Left -
Whitehall Chapel

Right -
The orignal range at Litharge is still in use.

Blackhall

Dating from at least the 17th century, the house is mentioned in a rental of 1663 together with a mill. Mr. & Mrs. G. Alexander bought the house, cottage and farm in 1939, making alterations in 1941. In the 1980s the group of buildings were awarded a grade II listed status.

Right - Blackhall sale details of June 24th 1851
Below - Blackhall c.1900

THE
BLACK HALL ESTATE,
In the Parish of Hexham, and
LANDS IN THE TOWN FIELDS OF HEXHAM,
NORTHUMBERLAND.

PARTICULARS AND CONDITIONS OF SALE
OF THE
FREEHOLD ESTATE
CALLED
BLACK HALL,
ABOUT FOUR MILES SOUTH FROM THE
MARKET TOWN OF HEXHAM,
IN NORTHUMBERLAND,
WHERE THERE IS A STATION ON THE NEWCASTLE AND CARLISLE RAILWAY.
THIS PROPERTY IS WELL ADAPTED FOR THE
SITE OF A GENTLEMAN'S RESIDENCE,
Being beautifully situated in a well Wooded and Picturesque Country, of which it commands fine Views to the South East and West.

Blackhall, Hexhamshire

plate 42

Left - Blackhall Cottage.
Date stone 1725 with the
initials J F on lintel.

Right - The engraved sundial
positioned on the front wall of
the house is dated 1714.
The J and F stand for the owner
John Featherstone.
The Swinburn family were the
owners during the 17th century.

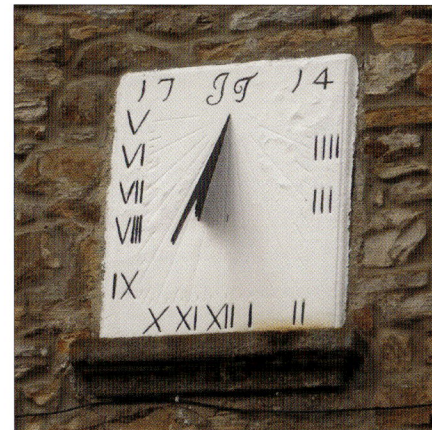

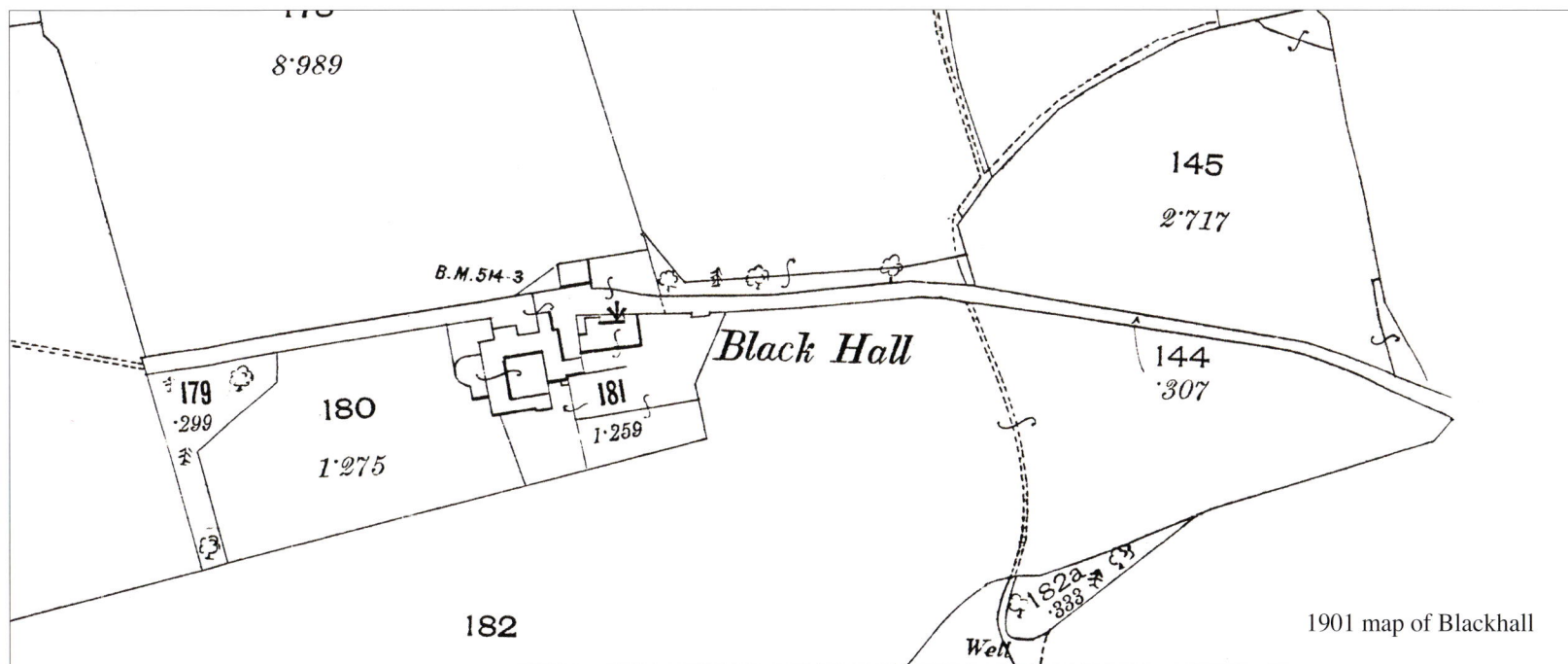

1901 map of Blackhall

HEXHAMSHIRE, NORTHUMBERLAND.

BLACKHALL ESTATE.

Particulars and Conditions of Sale

AND PLAN

OF THE DESIRABLE AND VALUABLE

FREEHOLD ESTATE

OF

BLACKHALL,

In the Parish of Hexham, in the County of Northumberland, beautifully situate amidst the picturesque scenery of the Devil's Water, about 4 miles south of the Town of Hexham.

Comprising an Excellent Private Dwelling-house, and a Farm Dwelling-house, with Commodious Farm Buildings, and 145 Acres of Land (of which about 113 acres are excellent Meadow and Pasture, and about 32 acres are Woodland) lying in a ring fence, sheltered on the north, south, and west sides by plantations and ornamental timber,

WHICH WILL BE OFFERED FOR

SALE BY PUBLIC AUCTION,

AT

THE ROYAL HOTEL, HEXHAM,

ON

TUESDAY, 13th AUGUST, 1901,

AT THREE O'CLOCK IN THE AFTERNOON,

BY

MESSRS. W. & T. T. IVESON,

AUCTIONEERS.

Copies of the Particulars and Conditions of Sale, with Plan, and any further information required, may be

Particulars of the sale of Blackhall 1901

Shooting party c.1910, Mr George Little standing in doorway

plate 43

The Little family from Harwood Shield c.1910

plate 44

FARM STOCK SALE
AT BLACKHALL, HEXHAMSHIRE
ON SATURDAY, MAY 2nd 1925.
WM. RUTHERFORD, F.A.I., on behalf
of the above Company, and favoured
with instructions from Messrs T. Carr and
Sons, will SELL BY AUCTION on the
above farm and date the following FARM-
ING STOCK, POULTRY, IMPLEMENTS,
& DAIRY UTENSILS, comprising:-
33 HEAD OF CATTLE
6 S.H. Cows, calved and to calve.
16 Irish Heifers, hay wintered.
1 S.H. Bull, 20 months old.
4 Stirks, 10 to 18 months old.
6 Finger Calves.
2 HORSES:
2 Draught Horses, quiet in all yokes.
IMPLEMENTS. – Self Binder, Swathe
Turner, Hay Rake, Hay Bogie, Single and
Double Grass Cutters, Drill Plough,
Ransome Plough, 2 pairs off Harrows,
Cultivator, 2 Coup Carts, Weighbridge and
Weights, Cake Crusher, Sheep Racks and
Troughs, Ware Troughs, Trap, 2 Sets of
Cart Harness, Trap Harness, Plough Chains
and Hand Tools, 2 Sets of Pulley Blocks,
Sack Truck and Hand Barrows, Winnowing
Machine, Stone Land Roller, Hay Sweep,
Meal Boxes, Sheep Netting, Ladders, etc.
DAIRY UTENSILS. – 2 Separators, Milk
Cooler, 2 Five-gallon Milk Churns, Barrel
Churn, Milk Cans, Pails, etc.
60 HEAD OF POULTRY
Mostly last year's Pullets.
REMARKS. – The Cattle at Blackhall are
well worthy of the attention of buyers, the
Cows being young and well bred, while the
hay-wintered Heifers are an especially fine
lot, being full of quality and condition and
needing very short keep. The Implements
are good.
Sale to commence at 12 noon.
REFRESHMENTS. TERMS – CASH.

plate 45

plate 46

Above - Photographs taken in 1939.

Below - As Blackhall looks today.

High Holmes

High Holmes 2012

Opposite page

Top -
High Holmes bastle dates from at least the
16th century; it is a listed Grade II building.

Lower left -
Interior of the farmhouse 1957.

Lower right -
Bastle fireplace.

Mr & Mrs John Carter purchased High
Holmes Farm in 1954; the house was
altered in the 1970s.
There was a tenement called The Holmes
mentioned in 1608.

Right -
Farmhouse in 1957 before alterations.

Above -
The altered house with new extension.

plate 47

plate 48

The Linnels

plate 49 The Linnels c.1890; Linnels farm in the background.

Painting of the Corn Mill c.1900

plate 50

The miller's house and corn mill, along with 14 acres were purchased by Mr R. B. Charlton in 1891. Plans were approved in 1897 for the additions and alterations to the house. Generations of the Charlton family have owned the Linnels for over a century.

The current mill still has most of its machinery in place, in addition to its millrace and sluice. It was last used around 1890 for milling oatmeal and is one of the oldest mills remaining in Northumberland.

A sign that used to be on display at the miller's house, when it was also being used as an inn, still exists: 'THOMAS TROTTER Licensed to RETAIL BEER on the Premises, TOBACCO'. (see opposite page)

After Thomas died his son John continued as the miller and innkeeper. The Linnels Inn would have been an ideal stopping place for drovers and travellers.

The new Linnels house was one of the first to be lit by electricity; the equipment used to supply this is still in place inside the mill building.

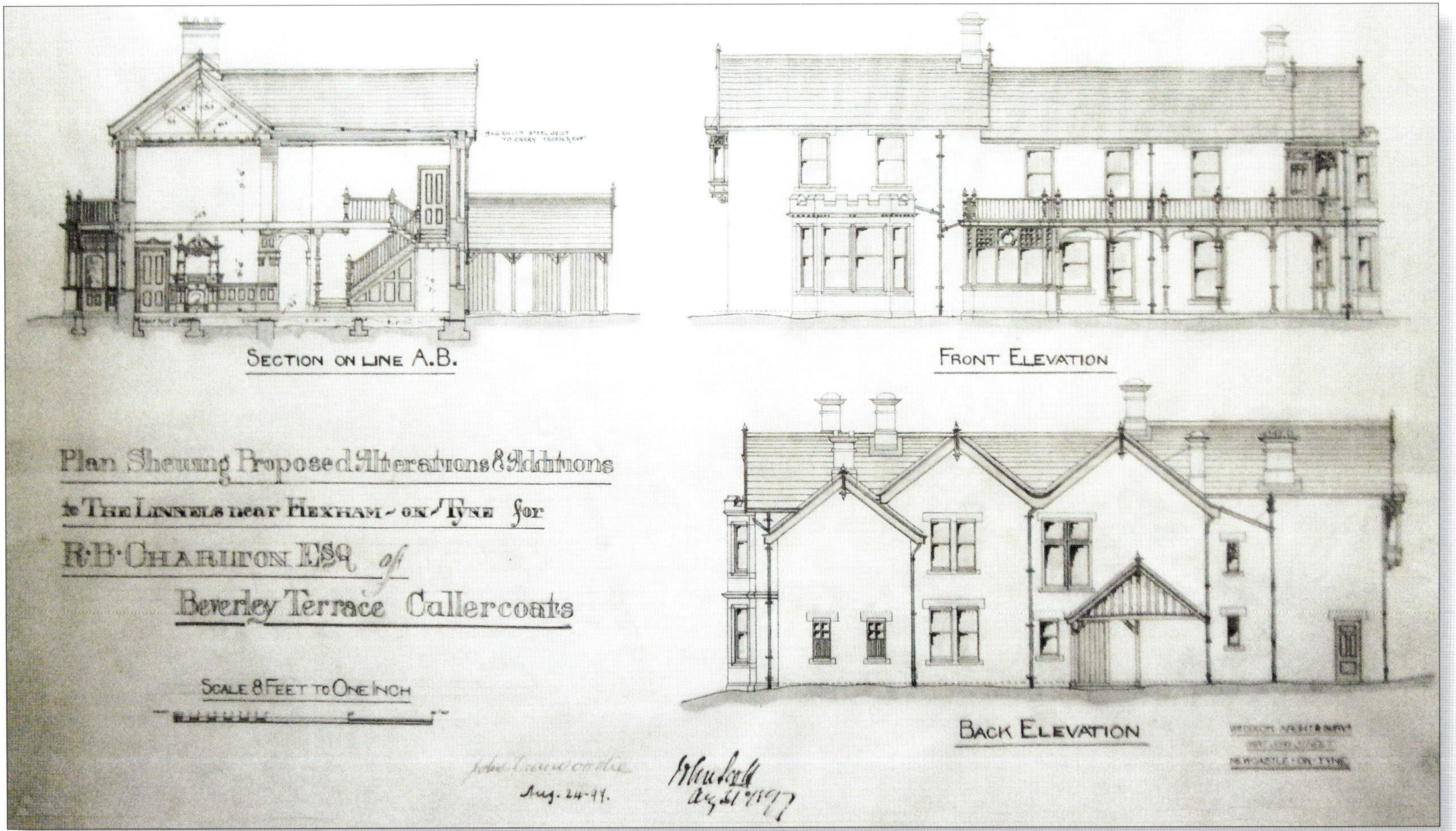
Section on line A.B.
Front Elevation
Plan Shewing Proposed Alterations & Additions
to The Linnels near Hexham-on-Tyne for
R.B. Charlton Esq of
Beverley Terrace Cullercoats
Scale 8 Feet to One Inch
Back Elevation
Aug. 24-97.

plate 51

Plans for the new Linnels 1897

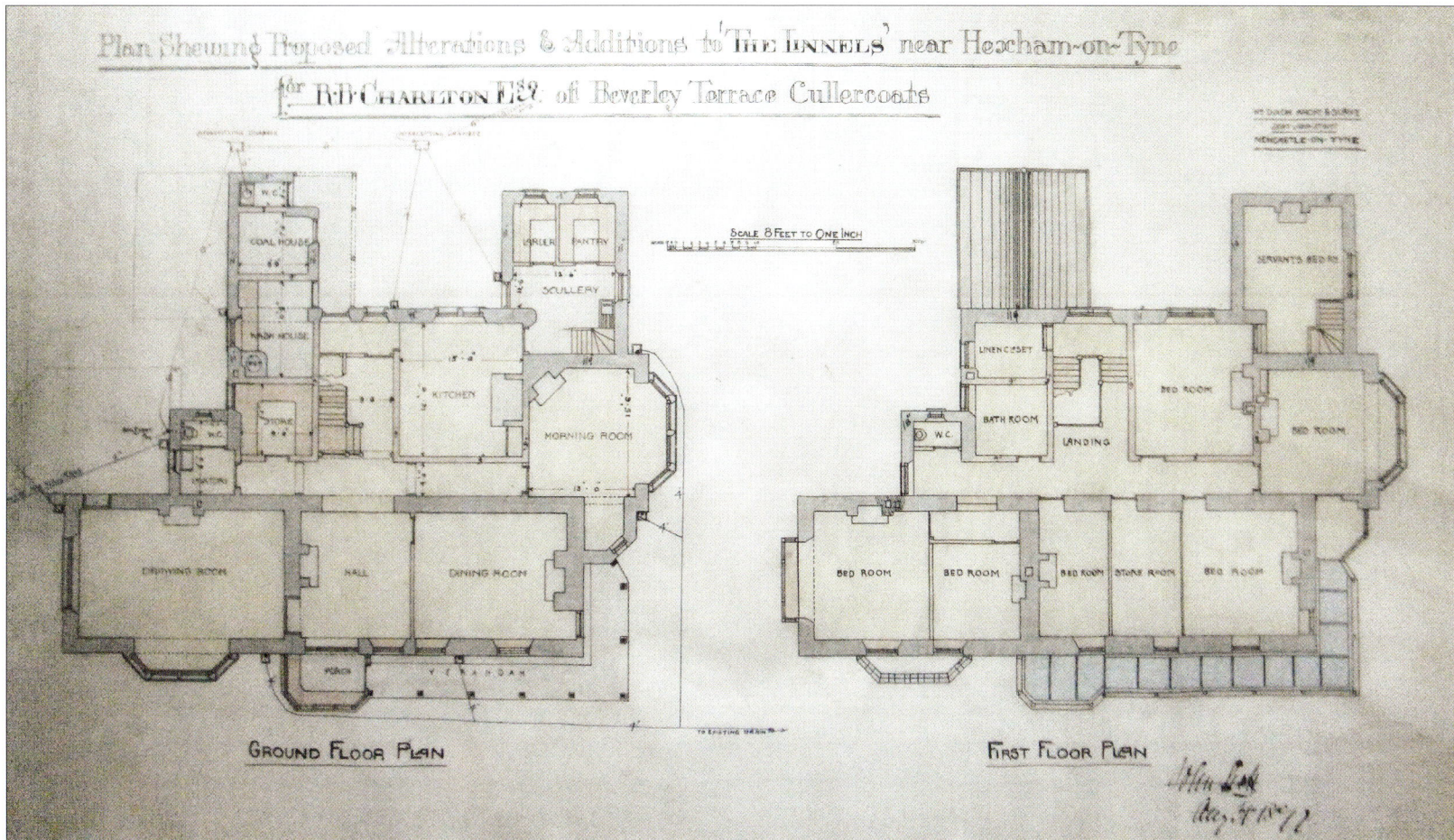

plate 52

plate 53

The Corn Mill c.1900

AT LINNOLDS BRIDGE NEAR HEXHAM.

Postcard dated 1910

plate 54

The Charlton wedding party at the Linnels   c.1910

The Linnels Bridge

There was a bridge over the Devil's Water from at least 1581. When it was rebuilt, possibly around 1700, the original stone tablet was incorporated within the parapet; the current bridge incorporates this original carved stone. Although now in very poor condition it is still partly legible on the outside edge facing north east.

At the Midsummer Quarter Session held in Hexham's Moot Hall in 1698, the owners of the Linnels Bridge, Benedict Errington of the Linnels and John Heron of Steel, were fined for allowing the bridge to be in bad repair.

GOD PRESARVE

WMFOIRA ERINGTON
BELLDETE THIS
BREGE OF LYME
AND STONE
1581

plate 55

The Linnels Bridge

Known far and wide for the beauty of its setting no less for its graceful proportions, the Linnels Bridge is famed in song and story. General regret will, therefore, be felt when it is known that on Tuesday last the eastern wall of the old bridge collapsed into the stream below, carrying with it the tablet which records the name of the builder. The bridge was built in 1581, for the inscription on the tablet, which in late years has been almost unreadable, so worn has the carving become, so states. The slab is of cunning workmanship. It had been graven without and within, but the inner face of the stone has long had most of its letters effaced. The Errington that built the bridge, one of the finest single spans in the country, was famed the "Chief of Beaufront" and though the male branch of that great family became extinct some half century ago, the late Lord Cromer, who married a daughter of Sir Rowland Stanley Errington, of Sandhoe, perpetuated the old name in his son, the present Lord Cromer. The bridge has carried the traffic of the district for centuries, but at last it has given signs of the ravages of time. The constant motor traffic has had the effect of steady outward pressure on the walls, as a matter of fact, the western wall, which carries the tablet, has only been in position by the interlocking stones, for the wall itself gradually became clear of the supporting bridge. The tablet is not damaged and the County Council authorities are going to replace the parapet wall and the tablet as nearly as may be as it was before the collapse.

Hexham Courant   January 28th 1928

Newbiggin

Newbiggin House, c.1900

The 'township' of Newbiggin is mentioned in a charter
dated May 8th 1355.

A mill is mentioned in 1608 in connection with the owner
Richard Thirlwall. The estate of Newbiggin remained
in the possession of the Thirlwall family for almost 150
years.

Cuthbert Surtees purchased Newbiggin in the mid 18th
century. He enlarged and extended the house; the sundial
is dated 1756 with the initials of Cuthbert and Dorothy.

plate 56

plate 57

Captain Leonard Wilson Atkinson, born June 24th 1836, was the owner of Newbiggin until he died in 1904.

SERVANTS BALL AT NEWBIGGIN

On New Year's day Captain Atkinson entertained the servants in his employ, together with their families and a number of their friends, to a dinner and ball. The apartments were beautifully decorated with evergreens and festoons. After a sumptuous repast had been partaken of, and which did great credit to Misses Dunn, Elliot, and Wanless, the health of Captain and the Misses Atkinson was proposed by Mr Pringle, and heartily responded to by the company. Subsequently, an adjournment was made to the ball room, the ball being led off by Mr J. Maughan, Nunsbrough, and Miss Johnson, Dotland Park. The entertainment was interspersed with songs. The company dispersed well pleased with their treat.

By 1803, the Atkinson family, descendants of Cuthbert Surtees, were the owners.

The balustrades, originally from the Theatre Royal, Newcastle, were added around 1900. A late 17th century plaster ceiling with central Tudor rose is still in place in the older part of the house. The house is listed as being of Architectural or Historical Interest (Grade II) with English Heritage.

Croquet at Newbiggin c.1860

The walled garden at Newbiggin

Right -
The outside of the walled garden.

Below -
The group of outbuildings attached to
outside of the walled garden.

Below right -
The greenhouse.

The garden walls, railings and outbuildings,
dating from the early 1800s, are also listed
Grade II. The greenhouse is positioned next
to the north wall, which would have been
heated by furnaces. A blacksmith's forge
was incorporated into the outbuildings.

Riddlehamhope

There has been a dwelling at Riddlehamhope in various forms since at least the 14th century. It may be one of the oldest settlements in Hexhamshire.

In 1897 the following was written about its early history:

'The old mansion house of Riddlehamhope is on the southern slope of the lofty fell, and overhangs the Beldon burn, an affluent of the Derwent. On November 8th 1333, the archbishop ordered his bailiff to arrest Richard Tully and Gilbert Cambe, tenants at Redelem, who had been excommunicated.
On the 21st September 1338, Edmund Howard, warden of the hospital of St. Giles of Kepyer, near Durham, did homage to the archbishop for South Ridlam in the liberty of Hexham, paying 40s a year. The place is very remote, however, and the tenants were probably unruly and independent. Its connection with Kepyer is also recorded in the survey of 1547, when it is described as "South Shield alias Ridelamehoppe".'

'A newly built tenement' was built round 1606, at 20s rent, suggesting that it either replaced the original building or was added to the settlement. This included an enclosed pasture with grazing for 300 sheep.

It has been suggested that one of the late 16th or early 17th century buildings may have been built as a bastle; one of the ruined older buildings had walls of over 1m thick, with a narrow opening, or slit vent, still visible on the north wall.

Due to its location, many baptisms, marriages and burials took place at Hunstanworth, Blanchland and Allendale in addition to Whitley Chapel. There were private burials at Riddlehamhope and Halliwell before, and possibly during, the 18th century.

The following are a few of the names of the occupants, although there would have been many more. It would seem that more than one family lived here at a time as different family names appear concurrently:

1547 – John Armestronge
1660 – Cicely Armistronge
1663 – Robert Bowman (rent £70)
1699 – Robert & William Bowman
1711 – John Robson
1724 – George Bowman
1724 to 1732 – William Bowman
1726 to 1740 - Joseph Ord
1730 – William Bowman
1730s to 1761 – Alexander Whaley
1741 – Robert Bell
1747 to 1750 - Isaac Burnhope

1750 to 1769 – William Whaley
1752 to 1768 – Robert Whaley
1773 – Joseph & Elizabeth Armstrong
1806 to 1816 – Robert & Ann Rowland
1817 – Robert & Mary Graham
1818 to 1823 – John & Elizabeth Graham
1825 – John & Margaret Oliver
1826 – William & Ann Armstrong
1827 – Joseph Arnstrong
1834 – John Armstrong
1834 – Ann Curry
1834 – Thomas Curry
1837 – Francis Pears
1839 – Abraham Bell
1840s – John & Mildred Bell
1850s – William Armstrong
1851 to 1855 - Anthony & Mary Hall
1858 – William Armstrong
1860s – William & Isabella Waggot
1870s – Isaac & Hannah Hardy
1870s – Elizabeth Gladstone
1880s – Oliver & Hannah Beattie
1880s – Elizabeth Graham
1886 – Philip Laing Esq.
1886 – William Avery (gardener)
1886 – William Fairless (gamekeeper)
1890s to 1911 census – Robert, Elizabeth Lowdon & family
1903 – owned by Rev. J W H Clavering
1903 – occupied by Brodie Cochran
1911 – Robert, Elizabeth, John William & Hannah Lizzie Lowdon
1926 to 1941 – Joseph Mole (gamekeeper) & family
1930s – J Cuthbert Forster

Cicely Armistronge's Will 1660

Memorandum that on or about the 21st Day of June last past to witt in the yeare of our lord god One thousand six hundred and sixty Cicely Armistronge of Ridlamhope in the County of Northumberland widow being sick in body but of good and perfect remembrance did in the presence of divers and sundry credible witnesses nuncupatively and by word of mouth declare with an intention and setled resolution to make her last will and testament as followeth. First she gave and bequeathed unto Reynold Armstronge one Cowe; Also she gave and bequeathed unto Jane Armestronge three kine. Also she gave and bequeathed unto Thomas Nevin the summe of fourteene pounds nineteene shillings and six pence which was in his owne hands, and also three pounds eighteene shillings and six pence which was then in the hands of one John Watson to be disposed of as he the said Thomas Nevin should thinke it meete and requisite. Which words, or the same in effect, now so uttered by the Testatrix in the presence and hearinge of the said Thomas Nevin and Jane Armestronge & other Witnesses.

CHRISTMAS CHARITY

On December 23rd C. J. Clavering Esq of Riddlehamhope, ordered a fat heifer to be distributed among the poor in the west quarter of Hexhamshire.

Newcastle Courant   January 3rd 1824

THUNDERSTORM

As Michael Anderson, herd to Messrs Armstrong, was riding with his wife on horseback between Riddlehamhope and Westburnhope, both horse and Mrs Armstrong were instantaneously struck dead, and what was remarkable, her husband remained unhurt!

Caledonian Mercury   Sept 11th 1824

GROUSE SHOOTING TO BE LET

The shooting over the Moors of Riddle-hamhope, Halywell and Harwoodshields, containing upwards of Two thousand acres.
Also the Mansion House (furnished), Garden, Pleasure grounds, Stable, Coach House at Riddlehamhope, the residence of the late Chas. John Clavering Esq. Riddlehamhope is situated four miles west of Blanchland, and twelve miles south-west of Hexham.
Mr. Abraham Bell, the Tenant, will show the house and grounds.

Newcastle Courant   April 12th 1839

SHOOTING BOX AND GROUSE SHOOT
TO BE LET

The furnished Shooting Box at Riddlehamhope,
containing Dining and Drawing rooms, Housekeepers
room, Butlers pantry, five Bedrooms and servant rooms,
two Stables, Dog kennel, Kitchen gardens
and Pleasure grounds, and seven good old grass fields
containing forty-two acres and the Right of shooting
over 2,200 acres of moorland, well stocked with grouse.
Riddlehamhope is well sheltered by plantations in
which there are laid out some very pleasant walks,
and is situated 4 miles west of Blanchland and 12 miles
south of Hexham.
William Armstrong, the woodkeeper, will show the
premises and further particulars may be known by
applying to Mr. Charles Armstrong, Axwell Park
Gateshead.

Newcastle Courant   January 31st 1851

Extract from " The Vasculum" Magazine 1935

NORTHERN NATURALISTS' UNION

The 22nd field meeting was held at Blanchland on June 15th and was very
successful, over 40 members attending and the weather being delightful. 19
members took the whole day and after exploring the river bank, where some
good mosses and liverworts were found, were most hospitably entertained to
lunch at Riddlehamhope by Mr and Mrs J. C. Forster. The wet shady banks of
the Beldon Burn near Riddlehamhope are favourable to the luxuriant growth
of Bryophytes. Miss Lobley found a variety of mosses not previously reported
from the area.

The collecting of ferns, mosses, flowers etc.
was a popular pastime in the 19th and early 20th
century. A vasculum was used to carry their plant
specimens.

plate 58

Riddlehamhope Shooting Lodge 1887
An extension was later added in 1920s to the east gable wall. Robert and Elizabeth Lowdon on left beside wall, Major Fisher, who rented Riddlehamhope in the late 19th century, is to be seen right of centre of photograph.

Plan dated 1817, with photographs taken from various aspects and dates, showing different parts of the 19th and 20th century buildings that made up Riddlehamhope. 1 & 2 - 1950s; 3 - 1930s; 4 & 5 - the standing ruin extension built after 1920; 6 - the ha-ha which is still visible.

barns

dog kennels

plate 59

Aerial photograph taken in 2009 showing the footprint of the former shooting lodge and the 20th century extension (no.5 on plan & on page 116).

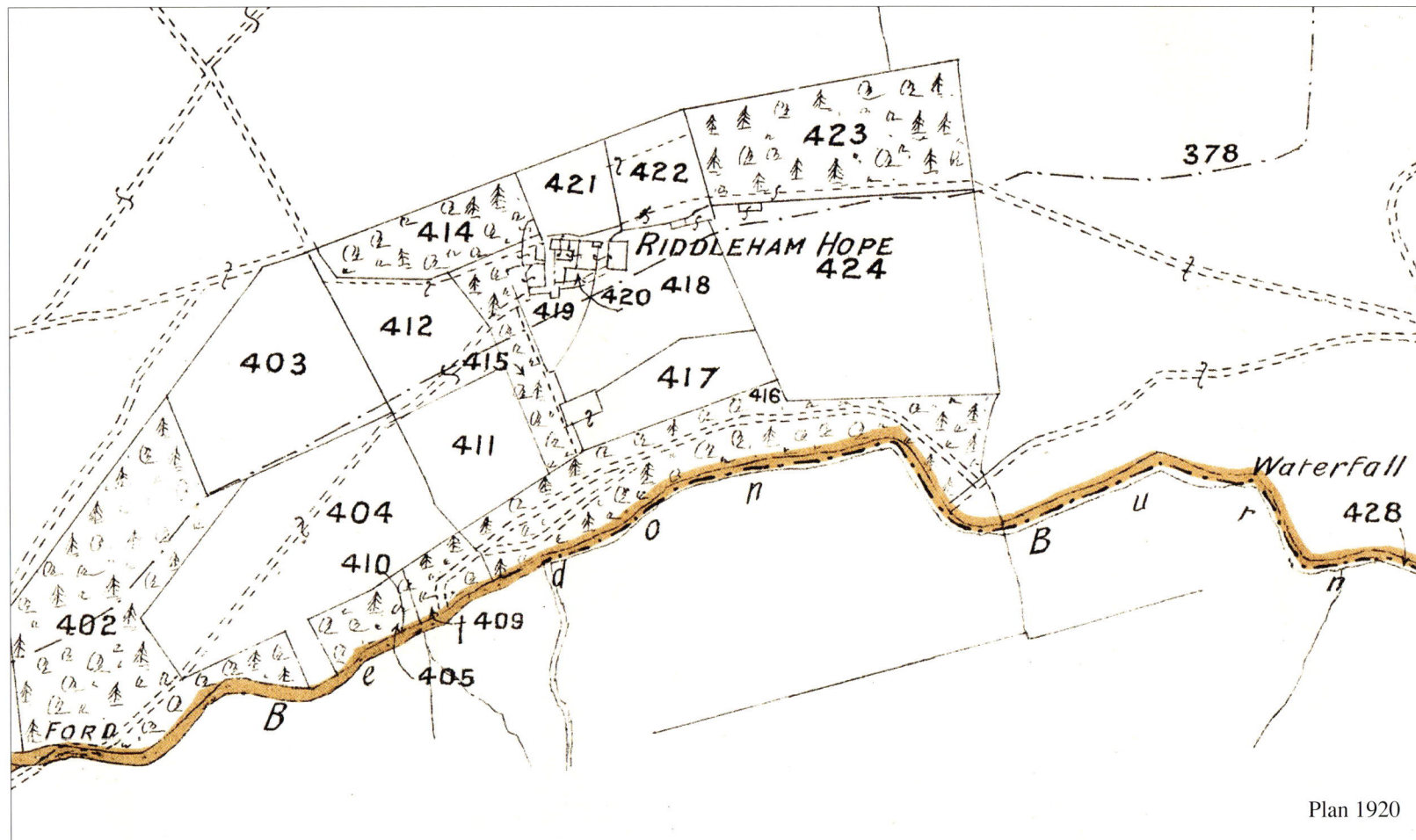

Plan 1920

Three **Reception** Rooms, **Gun** Room, Kitchen, Servants' Hall, Scullery, Larders **and Dairy**, Fourteen Bed and **Dressing** Rooms, Bath Rooms (H. and C.), and Lavatories with Out **Offices**, including Stabling for 4 **Horses**, **Byreing** for 6 Cattle, 2 Motor or Coach Houses, Petrol Store, 2 **Stone Built** Dog Kennels, with Yards **and Pig** and Poultry Houses, with Ornamental and Kitchen Gardens, **and a** Keeper's Cottage of three rooms with Pantry.

Description of the shooting lodge and outbuildings from the sales catalogue of 1920.
Note that the existing house has not been built at this time.

SOUTH NORTHUMBERLAND

Particulars, Plans and Conditions of Sale

OF

FREEHOLD AND COPYHOLD

Agricultural and Sporting Estates

Situate in the Parish of Hexham in the County of Northumberland, comprising

Riddlehamhope Shooting Lodge

with the Farm of

"HAREWOODSHIELD" and "HALLEYWELL"

and the detached Farms known as

"HACKFORD," and "EAST STOBBYLEE,"

For SALE BY AUCTION by

MESSRS. W. & T. T. IVESON,

AUCTIONEERS.

At the County Hotel, Newcastle-upon-Tyne,
on Monday, 28th June, 1920, at 2 p.m.

Solicitors :
Messrs. CLAYTON & GIBSON,
7, Grey Street,
Newcastle-upon-Tyne.

Land Agents :
Messrs. WM. T. BOLAM & SON,
4, Summerhill Terrace,
Westgate Road,
Newcastle-upon-Tyne.

Auctioneers :
Messrs. W. & T. T. IVESON,

LOT 1.

The Residential, Sporting and Pastoral Estate

of

"Riddlehamhope"

and

"Harewoodshield"

situate in the Parish of Hexham, in the County of Northumberland, 25 miles west of Newcastle-upon-Tyne, 10 miles south of Hexham, and 11 miles south west of Riding Mill.

The Lodge or Shooting Box of Riddlehamhope

contains

Three Reception Rooms, Gun Room, Kitchen, Servants' Hall, Scullery, Larders and Dairy, Fourteen Bed and Dressing Rooms, Bath Rooms (H. and C.), and Lavatories with Out Offices, including Stabling for 4 Horses, Byreing for 6 Cattle, 2 Motor or Coach Houses, Petrol Store, 2 Stone Built Dog Kennels, with Yards and Pig and Poultry Houses, with Ornamental and Kitchen Gardens, and a Keeper's Cottage of three rooms with Pantry.

All the above are in hand.

Adjoining the premises are six Grass Fields containing 17·226 acres or thereabouts. These fields and the Cottage are let and occupied as mentioned below but the sporting rights over the fields are in hand.

HAREWOODSHIELD FARM

with

Halleywell

comprises

2,378·367 acres or thereabouts of sound Grass and Moorland.

The Farm House

contains

Two Sitting Rooms, Front and Back Kitchens, Dairy, Pantry, Wash House and Coal House, and Six Bedrooms.

THE FARM BUILDINGS

include

Byreing for 34 Cattle, Stabling for 7 Horses, Wool Loft, Granary, 2 Cart Sheds, Keb House, Motor or Coach House, Hay Shed, and Barn, 2 Pig Houses, Joiner's Shop, Pot House, and Poultry House.

and

At HALLEYWELL

SHEPHERD'S COTTAGE

containing Sitting Room, Kitchen, Back Kitchen, Pantry, and 2 Bedrooms, with 1 Horse Stable, Byre for 8 Cattle, Hay Loft, Cart Shed, and Piggeries.

Woodlands of 33·853 acres are in hand.

3

Left and above - plan and details of the sale of Riddlehamhope 1920. The vendor was Charles W. Napier-Clavering of Axwell Park, Co. Durham.

Extract from
NORTH COUNTRY HUNTING
by N. W. Apperley
written in the late 1800s

10th November, Riddlehamhope - Mr Richard Johnson's Trencher-fed Pack of Foxhounds.

There was deep snow on the ground and the weather was very cold. The previous evening I had been to a dinner party at Thornton Salvin's of Croxdale Woodhouse, which was kept up with champagne and smoke till the small hours of the morning; so instead of going to bed I went up to the Durham railway station and got "Farren," the night stationmaster, to rig me up a bed with 1st class railway cushions before the fire in the ladies waiting room, and there I slept comfortably till he called me at 6 a.m., and I left by the 6.18 train for Stanhope, where I was met by a hired four-wheeled dog-cart and pair, and drove over the open mountains and moors for a distance of 10 miles. The cold was intense and snow very deep; in fact if it had not been for the posts which indicated where the road was, it would have been impossible to find it.
The poor lad who drove went constantly to sleep, if not employed in blowing on his fingers, and I had to keep constant watch upon him and dig his ribs to wake him up, or a ditch would have been our destination. We came across several heavy drifts, and the snow was also drifting heavily at the time. I saw several grouse on the road, which were in easy gunshot from the trap. Riddlehamhope is Mr. R. S.Johnson's shooting box for his moor, and, objecting to his keepers shooting and trapping foxes, it being much against the grain of a foxhunter to do so, he prohibited them doing anything of the sort.

The snow was from 18 inches to 2 feet deep, consequently no one arrived but myself, and that after considerable trouble, I arriving at my destination at 11 a.m., having travelled since 6.18 a.m. The whole journey was performed without food of any description, so when I did sit down to breakfast I ate a whole grouse and a dish of bacon etc.
Riddlehamhope is a nice old shooting box, and could not be better filled than by our host, whose hospitality exceeds anything I know; his generosity and kindness are unbounded.

Right - Falconer Major C Hawkins Fisher rented Riddlehamhope in the late 1880s & 90s.
Below - William Rutherford, assistant falconer, the 'Princess'; Major Fisher with 'Lady Jane Grey' and James Rutford, falconer, with 'Lundy'.

Mr J. C. Forster and gamekeeper Joe (Jack) Mole, 1930s.

20th century extension (see page 116), note earlier house wall on left.

View on the buildings from the north west (see page 116).

View from the south west (see page 116).

Above - One of the attic bedrooms.

Top right - View from sitting room window.

Below - First floor bedroom fireplace.

Above - View from an attic window.

Below left - Staircase up to first floor.

Below - The 1920's kitchen range.

Above - View from the west with all that remains
of the house in the foreground.
Below and right - West wall with the different
roof lines visable. The extension was attached to
east gable of the old house.

Above - The south side with the wall of the older
building visable to the left.
Below - View from the old garden.
(The ruin, which is on private land, is currently in a
dangerous condition and is being demolished.)

Riddlehamhope Memories

by Nancy Graham (nee Lowdon)

I have been asked many times what I know of Riddlehamhope so I will try to put down on paper any details that I have.

My grandparents, Robert and Elizabeth Lowdon, lived there in the early years of the 20th century. Grandfather was gamekeeper / gardener / handy-man and grandmother was caretaker. Their employer was Mr J. C. Forster of Sloane Square, London.

My father, John Lowdon, also worked there from leaving school until he went into the army and again until 1920.

After grandfather retired, I believe Joe Mole was gamekeeper. In the nineteen thirties Jack and Kitty Mole lived at Riddlehamhope and had the same duties as my grandparents. Their home was in the 'bothy' which was up stone steps.

For the two summers of 1938 and 1939 my brother, Tommie Lowdon, worked there. The employer was still Mr Forster. Tommie's wage was £1-10-2d per week, no cost of living increase for the second year! Out of this he paid Mrs Mole 17 shillings board.

The 'gentry' came part time during the early part of the summer and lived there full time during the grouse shooting season. They usually brought about ten members of staff, housekeeper, cook, maids etc. They came in two huge cars – a Sunbeam, built like a tank, and a Wolsley.

Tommie's duties included sawing sticks, getting coals in, gardening, mending shooting butts, keeping the road through Beldon Cleugh in good repair and any other maintenance jobs. During the shooting season he was in charge of the game larder. The grouse were hung by their heads on racks and when the body came away from the head they were deemed ready to eat.

On shooting days the food, whisky, wine and beer were taken out by horse and cart, often to Hallywell; there was a bottle of beer for each of the adult beaters and a bottle of lemonade for the boys.

The staff were given time off on Wednesdays. I suppose some went on alternate weeks. They were taken to Blanchland to catch a bus to spend the day in Newcastle and were met from the bus at night.

Mr & Mrs Forster often went to Hexham on Tuesdays. Tommie went with them to open the gates and was given 4/-6d to spend on lunch. He made a profit those days as a packet of chips cost very little.

Mr Mole was always in charge of cleaning the guns. In season he grew daffodils and tulips and they were boxed up and sent to Mr Forster's house in London.

Most of the groceries were bought in Blanchland, hence the need to keep that road in good repair. Mr Mole kept a house cow and bees and there would always be garden produce available.

The following letters show how employers and employees addressed each other at that time.

Dear Lowdon,

I am sending you £3-10-0d. on account of your wages and will settle with you when I come North.

Yours truly,
J. C. Forster

Mr Forster,
Dear Sir,

Thanks for the remittance of £3-10/- received on May 26th. I am your humble servant,

J. T. Lowdon

(It is interesting to note that Mr Forster's letter was actually posted at Folkestone on May 25th 1938 and received at Riddlehamhope the next day.)

Robert Lowdon

Stotsfold Hall

plate 60

Stotsfold Hall 1980s

TO BE LET,

For 12 Years, and entered to at May-day first,

STOTSFOLD FARM, situated in Hexhamshire, about five Miles South from Hexham; and containing 284 Acres of Land, together with several Stints upon the undivided Part of Hexhamshire Common. The Servant upon the Farm will shew the same; and further Particulars may be known on Application to Jasper Gibson, Solicitor, Hexham.—October 21, 1812.

Stotsfold Farmhouse 1960

SALE OF VALUABLE FARMING STOCK,
IMPLEMENTS, &c., &c.

MR LIDDLE FORSTER has the pleasure to
announce that he has received instructions
from Mr George Robson, who is declining Farming,
to SELL BY AUCTION, at STOTSFOLD, Hexhamshire, on Wednesday, April 2, 1879, the whole of his
Valuable FARMING STOCK, HAY, IMPLE-
MENTS, &c., comprising –
DRAUGHT HORSES.
1 Bay Mare, aged.
1 Bay Mare, 4 Years Old.
1 Two years-old Filly, by the "Chief".
CATTLE
3 S.H. Cows, calved and close at calving
2 S.H. Heffers, May calvers
4 Two-years-old S.H. Heifers
6 One-year-old S.H. Steers and Heifers
5 H.B. Heifers, part of them in calf
SHEEP
40 Blackfaced young Ewes and Gimmers, in Lamb
by a Leicester Tup
5 Mule Gimmers, in Lamb by a Leicester Tup
20 Male Hoggs, very fresh
IMPLEMENTS, Etc.
1 Two-horse Thrashing Machine, 1 Two-horse
Reaping and Mowing Machine, American Hay
Rake, 2 Coup Carts, 2 Sets of Cart and Plough
Harness, Double Iron Plough, Single Iron Plough,
Turnip Scuffler, Iron Double Harrow, Seed Harrow,
Double Turnip Drill, Oak Roller, Stone Roller,
Turnip Cutter, Dipping Tub, 34 good Hurdles,
Winnowing Machine, Sacks, Pokes, Gripes, Rakes,
Forks, Shovels, a quantity of useful old Iron, 1
Barrel Churn and Milk-vessel, &c., &c. Also, a
quantity of Regent Potatoes, a few Tons of well-
won New Land Hay, to be consumed on the pre-
mises, and the Over-eatage of upwards of Two
Hundred Acres of Seeds, Grass Fields, Allotment
and Plantation Lands, until the 13th day of May,
1879.
The Sale to commence at 12 o'clock, at Noon.
Terms – Cash.
March 17th, 1879.

In 1547 *Stobfolde* belonged to Cuthbert Ord; by
1608, *Scottfouldes* was held by John Ord when
it was worth £3 3s 4d a year. In 1637 Stotsfold,
with 148 acres of freehold land and 24 stints on
Hexhamshire common, was owned by George
Gibson; the farm stayed in the ownership of the
Gibson family and their descendants until 1800
when it was sold to John Robson of Allenheads
Mill. His daughter Dorothy Lynn and her husband Peacock inherited the farm.

*We hear that Stotsfold Farm, recently
purchased by Mr. Wilkinson of Riverdale,
Bellingham, has changed owners and now
passes into the hands of the Misses Mounsey of Sunderland, who, we believe, intend
erecting a fine and costly mansion thereon.*
Hexham Courant   May 25th 1901

plate 61   Lucy E Mounsey

plate 62   Mary E Mounsey

Extracts from Katherine Backhouse's
'Dukes House Journal'
Katherine was married to Edward Backhouse
Mounsey, brother of Lucy and Mary.

1901

*Augt. 13th Came to Dukes House & were joined
on the 16th by Lucy E. & Mary E. Mounsey who
staid with us till the 4th of October, devoting a
good deal of time to seeing after the laying out of
their new estate at Stotsfold, & making arrangements for building their new house there. They
had their own carriage &c. in the town, & we
had our landau here for the first time which we
found much more convenient than the wagonette.
I went to Stotsfold for the first time on the 24th.*

*On the 20th Edwd & Rachel Mounsey came,
wishing to see Stotsfold. On the 5th Oct. we sent
the carriage to bring Mrs Josephine Butler from
Corbridge where she was staying, to dine with
us. She looked feeble and much aged, but was
pleased to renew her memories of riding over this
part of the country with her Father, John Grey of
Dilston.*

1902

*Augt. 12th Tuesday
Satisfactory progress has been made with their
house at Stotsfold, which is just ready for roofing.*

*Came in Motor Car from Darlington in about
3 ½ hours, via Durham, Lanchester, Ebchester,
Riding Mill, & Corbridge. Next day visited Stotsfold, & were charmed with its appearance & the
effect of the grounds.*

*July 30th. Lucy E. & Mary E. Mounsey left Dukes
House on the 30th July, having much appreciated
their stay there; to begin life at Stotsfold.*

1903

*Augt. 5 Wed.
On the 11th paid my first visit to Stotsfold taking
lunch there with Gertrude and Miss Thurgood.
Lucy E. & Mary E. Mounsey are inhabiting one
end of the house, the main staircase &c. not yet
being finished. On the 1st Sept. we had a call
from Alfred, Basil, & Jennett Backhouse, with a
Miss Knight who had come over in their motor-
car from Dryderdale to lunch at Stotsfold, &
called here on their way back. Some of us tried a
drive in it as far as the gate & back. It had a very
shakey motion though pleasant in some ways.*

*On the 1st Sept, Carie Mounsey went to Stotsfold,
returning here for one night. On Thursday the
17th M. Clark, L. Gardiner & I paid an afternoon
call at Stotsfold much to their surprize. It was a
lovely day.*

1904

*Augt. 3
Jon & V. M. A. Hodgkin with their daughter Mary
came to dinner on the 19th Augt. on their way
from Stotsfold. I took Elsie & Daisy to tea at
Stotsfold on the 25th & saw the house finished for
the first time. Wilfred & Charlotte & Josephine
Mounsey came on the 29th from Stotsfold, Aimee
& I spent 3 nights at Stotsfold from 3rd to 6th
Sept, very pleasantly.*

Misses Lucy and Mary Mounsey built the hall as
a summer residence away from their family home
at Hendon Hill, Sunderland; they came from a
Quaker family of ship builders.
Stotsfold Hall was designed by architect Wm.
Dixon of Newcastle in 1898; the plans included
a large reception hall, library, three reception
rooms, seven bedrooms, two bedrooms, a cellar
and many other smaller rooms.
In the 1911 census two members of staff were
resident: 37 year old Jane Foster was parlour
maid and the house maid was 16 year old Margaret Clark. 49 year old William Oliver was the
gardener.
Lucy died in 1922; her sister Mary continued to
live at Stotsfold until she died on February 26th
1940.

*Mr Backhouse Mounsey. I may also say that
he is not unknown in this district, seeing that
he is a nephew of Mrs Backhouse of Duke's
House and has often visited there, while his
sisters, the Misses Mounsey, are the owners
of the stately mansion that is nearing completion on the estate they recently purchased at
Stotsfold, Hexhamshire, and in which they
have taken up their residence for the first time
this week.*

Hexham Courant   March 1st 1902

Right -
The Stotsfold Hall estate, which included
the house, farm and Stotsfold Lodge, was
offered for sale by auction on 11th June
1940 at the Royal Hotel, Hexham.
The contents were sold by auction at
Stotsfold on the 5th, 6th & 7th June.

PLAN AND PARTICULARS

OF THE

FREEHOLD PROPERTY AND LAND

KNOWN AS

STOTSFOLD HALL ESTATE,

STEEL, HEXHAMSHIRE,

NORTHUMBERLAND,

COVERING AN AREA OF

285 ACRES

OR THEREABOUTS,

With 24 Stints on Hexhamshire (High Quarter) Stinted Pasture,

TO BE OFFERED FOR

SALE BY AUCTION

(Unless previously sold privately),

Subject to Conditions of Sale, which will then be read,

On TUESDAY, 11th JUNE, 1940,

BY

Messrs. WALLHEAD, SMITH & CO., F.A.I.

AT THE

ROYAL HOTEL, HEXHAM,

AT 3 P.M. PRECISELY

Permits to view may be obtained on application to the Auctioneers :—

Messrs.
WALLHEAD, SMITH & CO.,
Auctioneers, Valuers & Estate Agents,
7, PRIESTPOPPLE,
HEXHAM.
Telephone 302.
Also at 84, Pilgrim St., Newcastle-upon-Tyne. Tel. 25812.
75, West Street, Gateshead. Tel. 72197.

Messrs.
STEEL MAITLAND & BYERS,
Solicitors,
51, JOHN STREET,
SUNDERLAND.
Telephone 3038.

PARTICULARS OF SALE.

THE

STOTSFOLD HALL ESTATE

is situated about 12 miles south of Hexham in beautiful health-giving country, 900 feet above Sea Level.

THE RESIDENCE

is substantially built, of stone and was erected in 1902. It stands in well laid out Grounds having an area of 15 acres or thereabouts, approached by a carriage drive and commands extensive views over the Hexhamshire Moors and charming country. The accommodation is as follows :—

ON THE GROUND FLOOR :

Lobby entrance Hall with Cloakroom and W.C., Lounge Hall with fireplace, Dining Room, Drawing Room, Composite Room, bath and W.C., Maid's Sitting Room, Kitchen, Scullery, Dairy, etc.

ON THE FIRST FLOOR :

Which is approached by a main staircase and back staircase. 7 Principal Bedrooms, 4 Maids' Bedrooms, 2 Bathrooms and 3 W.C.'s Linen Cupboard and Housemaid's Pantry.

ON THE SECOND FLOOR :

Attic Bedroom, Boxroom and Tank Cupboard.

Attached to the house is a well-equipped modern Laundry on two floors. The Residence is of modern design, is centrally heated throughout and has private Electric Light Plant.

OUTBUILDINGS

These comprise Gardener's House and Stabling, Chauffeur's House, two Garages for four Cars, Potting Sheds, Tool Houses, etc.

STOTSFOLD FARM

Comprising Stone Built House of 7 Rooms, Bathroom and W.C., Kitchen, Pantry, Dairy, etc. Usual outside domestic offices. Outbuildings include Byres, Stabling, Barn, Meal House, Pig Styes, Hay and Implement Sheds, etc. About 211 Acres of Meadow and Pasture Land, also 24 Stints on Hexhamshire (High Quarter) Stinted Pasture. Let to Mr. G. E. Bell (who has been in aoccuption over 50 years.) Rent £100 per annum.

Stotsfold Hall Estate Catalogue 1940

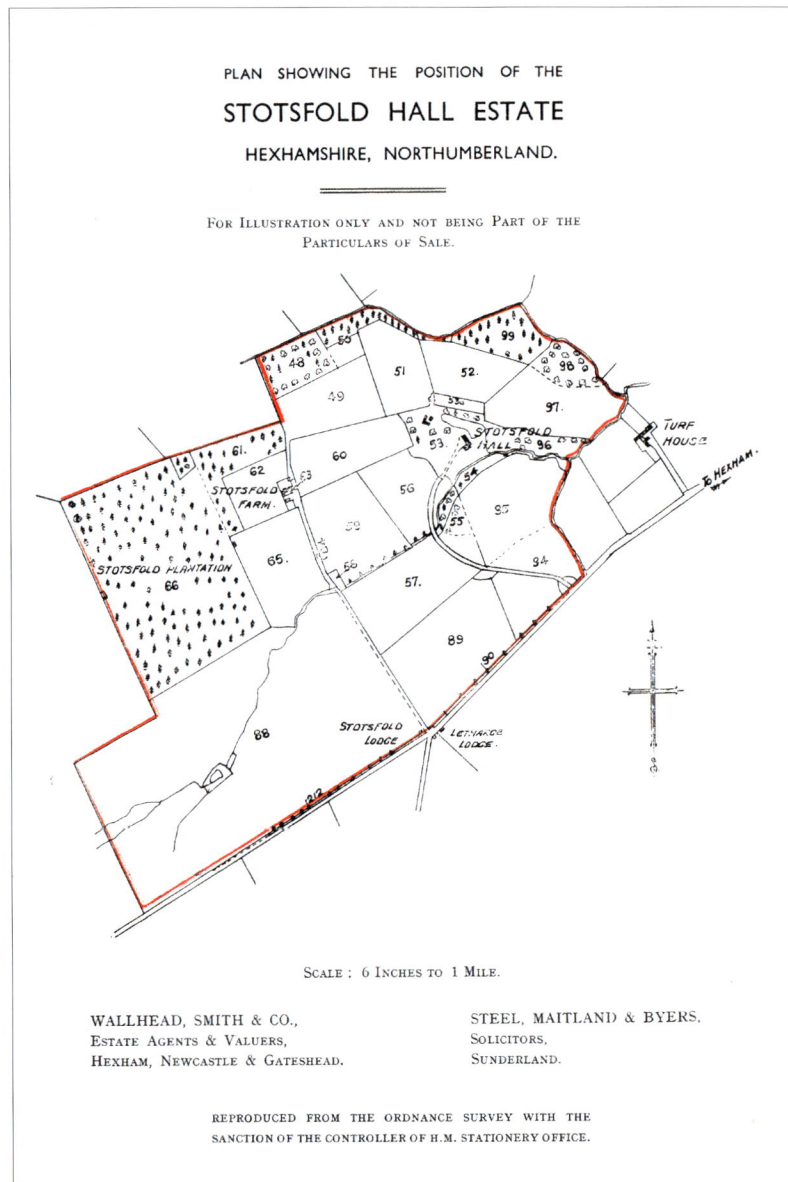

PLAN SHOWING THE POSITION OF THE

STOTSFOLD HALL ESTATE

HEXHAMSHIRE, NORTHUMBERLAND.

FOR ILLUSTRATION ONLY AND NOT BEING PART OF THE
PARTICULARS OF SALE.

SCALE : 6 INCHES TO 1 MILE.

WALLHEAD, SMITH & CO.,
ESTATE AGENTS & VALUERS,
HEXHAM, NEWCASTLE & GATESHEAD.

STEEL, MAITLAND & BYERS.
SOLICITORS,
SUNDERLAND.

REPRODUCED FROM THE ORDNANCE SURVEY WITH THE
SANCTION OF THE CONTROLLER OF H.M. STATIONERY OFFICE.

Above - 1940 Plan of Estate
Right - Catalogue of house contents

THE STOTSFOLD ESTATE
STEEL, HEXHAMSHIRE,
Situate about 12 miles South of Hexham.
In beautiful Health-Giving Country—900 feet above Sea level.
re Miss M. E. MOUNSEY, deceased.

The above desirable Freehold Estate, area about 285 acres or thereabouts, will be offered for Sale by Auction at the Royal Hotel, Hexham, on Tuesday, the 11th June, 1940,

AT 3 O'CLOCK IN THE AFTERNOON.   It comprises :—

STOTSFOLD HALL (with Vacant possession on completion) :   A most substantial stone built residence, containing 3 Reception Rooms, Maid's Sitting Room, Kitchen, etc. on Ground Floor ; 7 Principal Bedrooms, 4 Maid's Bedrooms, 2 Bathrooms, etc. on First Floor ; and Attic Bedroom, Boxroom, etc. above, also well-equipped Laundry on two floors. Outbuildings include Gardener's House, Stabling, Chauffeur's House, Garages, Potting Sheds, Tool Houses, etc.
Beautifully situate in well laid out Grounds, having an area of 15 acres or thereabouts and commanding extensive views over the Hexhamshire Moors and charming country.

STOTSFOLD FARM. : Well built House of 7 Rooms, Bathroom, Kitchen, Dairy, etc.   Outbuildings including Byres, Stabling, Barn, Mealhouse, Pig Styes, Hay and Implement Sheds, etc.
About 200 Acres of Meadow and Pasture Land, also 24 Stints on Hexhamshire Common. Tenant, Mr. Bell. Rental, £100 per annum.

STOTSFOLD LODGE : Detached Stone built House of 4 Rooms and Scullery. Usual outoffices and good Garden. At present in occupation of Mr. Clark, Estate Woodman.

PLANS and further particulars may be had on application to the Auctioneers.

SOLICITORS : Messrs. STEEL, MAITLAND & BYERS, 51, John Street, Sunderland.

CATALOGUE
of the HOUSEHOLD FURNISHINGS & APPOINTMENTS of
STOTSFOLD HALL, HEXHAMSHIRE,
To be offered for Sale by Auction on the Premises on Wednesday, Thursday and Friday, 5th, 6th and 7th JUNE, 1940,
commencing each day at 11 o'clock.
Goods on View, day prior to and mornings of Sale.

ORDER OF SALE.
FIRST DAY :   Principal Furnishings, Glass and China, Silver and E.P. Goods, Cutlery, Books, etc.
SECOND DAY : Bedroom Furnishings, Bedding and Soft Goods.
THIRD DAY :   Bedroom and Kitchen Furnishings, Summer Houses and Outside Effects.

Auctioneers :
WALLHEAD, SMITH & CO., F.A.I.
OFFICES : No. 7, Priestpopple, Hexham. (Tel. No. Hexham 302).
No. 84, Pilgrim Street, Newcastle-upon-Tyne. (Tel No. 25812).
No. 75, West Street, Gateshead. (Tel. No. 72197).

PRICE, 6d. EACH.

9

DRAWING ROOM—continued.

Lot

143 Mahogany Octagonal Table with platform under.

144　　do.　　do.　　do.

145 **Walnut Oriental Hexagonal Table inlaid with Mother of Pearl.**

146 **Mahogany Folding Side-Table.**

147 **Mahogany 4ft. 6ins. Writing Desk with Leather Top.**

148 Deal Table with two Drawers.

149 Deal Table.

150 **Mahogany 6 ft. Bookcase with glazed front and Cupboards below.**

151 **6 ft. 3 ins. Mahogany Sideboard fitted 3 drawers and 3 Cupboards.**

152 Mahogany Chiming Mantel Clock.

153 Pair Water Colours in Oak Frames by M. B. Bigland.

154 Pair Water Colours by A. Lamplaugh.

155 Pair Water Colours by M. B. Bigland.

156 Pair Water Colours by Bigland.

157 Pair Water Colours in Gilt Frames by Ernest Stuart.

158 1 Oil painting by W. B. Scott and 3 Water Colours.

159 5 Engravings.

160 3 Mohair Mats (worn).

161 2 Small Axminster Hearth Mats.

162 2 Axminster Mats.

163 Oriental Hearth Rug and 1 other.

164 Large Wool Mat, 9 ft. by 3 ft. 9 ins.

165 2 Skin Mats.

166 Large Skin Mat.

167　　do.

168 Pair Curtains, 9 ft. high by 8 ft.

11

TEA CHINA, DINNER WARE, etc.—continued.

Lot

194 " Queens Green " Tea and Dinner Service comprising :-
15 Soup Plates, 13 Dinner Plates, 11 Dessert Plates, 7 Fruit Dishes, 15 Small Plates, 21 Saucers, 14 Cups, 5 Egg Cups, 2 Cruets, 3 Small Jugs, 2 Hot Water Jugs and Sugar Basin, Fruit Dish, etc.—124 pieces.

195 Blue and White Breakfast Service :—12 Cups, 12 Saucers and 12 Plates, 6 Egg Cups, 5 Jugs, 2 Sugar Basins and 4 large Plates.—53 pieces.

196 Blue and White Breakfast Service :—12 Plates, 12 Saucers, 10 Cups, 6 Egg Cups, 1 Sugar Basin, 3 Jugs, 5 large Plates.—49 pieces.

197 Blue and White Tea Service :—12 Plates, 12 Saucers, 12 Cups, 2 Bread Plates, Sugar and Cream and 3 Jugs. 43 pieces.

198 Blue and White Tea Service :—12 Plates, 12 Saucers 12 Cups, 2 Bread Plates, Sugar and Cream, and Hot Water Jug.—41 pieces.

199 Blue and White Dinner Service :—4 Meat Plates, Soup Tureen, Vegetable Dish, 3 Gravy Boats, 3 Soup Plates, etc.—22 pieces. (Parts damaged.)

200 Blue and White Dinner Service :—6 Meat Plates, 24 Dinner Plates, 24 Dessert Plates, 4 Vegetable Dishes, Gravy Boat and 2 Sauce Bowls.—63 pieces.

201 Blue and White Dinner Service :—8 Meat Plates, 19 Dinner Plates, 15 Dessert Plates, 6 Vegetable Dishes, 2 Gravy Bowls, Sauce Boat and Soup Tureen.—56 pieces.

DINING ROOM.

202 Copper Kettle on Stand.

203 Small Mantel Clock, etc.

204 Chiming Mantel Clock in Walnut.

205 3 Small Fire-guards and Fire-irons.

206 Large Fire-guard, Coal Scuttle and pair Bellows.

207 Small Folding Chair and Luggage Stand.

Horse Power

Travelling stallions were a regular sight until the early 20th century. They would be led around pre-arranged routes to cover mares. The stallions would often stay at inns where farmers could take their mares; see advert left.

Farmers prefered to use the larger breeds, such as Clydesdales, to produce the next generation of working horses.

The Linnel Stud specialised in breeding ponies, in particular Dales and Hackneys, in the early 20th century but are now better known for their famous Fell ponies.

Linnel Pony Stud
Forthcoming Dispersal Sale   August 5th 1919

An important sale of the entire stud of high class Dales and Hackney ponies, the property of Mr. R. B. Charlton, will take place at Hexham Auction Mart on Tuesday, August 5th.

It will be the most important sale of Dales ponies yet held in this district. Mr. Charlton was one of those chiefly instrumental in popularising the breed and establishing a stud book, and has been for some years an enthusiastic breeder of this now distinctive and great dual purpose pony.

The young stock show great promise, and the yearling colt 'Linnel Heather' is without question one of the best of the registered Dales pony colts and is likely to make a great stallion. 'Linnel Comet', the six-year old stallion, is just finishing his second season as one of the Board of Agriculture premium sires, and is probably the most valuable Dales pony living. The brood mares are an ideal lot, and in the saddle and harness ponies include 'Linnel Lady', a noted show pony.

A prize winning Clydesdale stallion; the type favoured by the majority of farmers in the area.

ROUTE FOR 1919.

TUESDAY, April 29th, & Weekly for Season.
Leave Hexham 1 p.m. by Slaley to Whittonstall over night.

WEDNESDAY:—Ebchester, Shotley Bridge, Blackhill, (11-30 to 2-30) Leadgate to Lanchester over night.

THURSDAY:—Maiden Law, Stanley, Burnopfield, Rowlands Gill, Winlaton to Black Horse Hotel, Greenside, over night.

FRIDAY:—Wylam, Ovingham, (Bridge End Inn, from 11-30 to 2-30) Ovington Village, South Acomb, Stocksfield to Mr. Dryden's Farm, Broomhaugh, over night.

SATURDAY:—Riding Mill, Corbridge, Stagshaw & to Hexham.

MONDAY:—Stand at Blue Bell Stables, Hallgate, Hexham, or meet Mares by appointment.

GROOM—Mr. ARTHUR HESLOP,
7, St. George's Road, HEXHAM.

TERMS.

Groom's Fee, 2/6 for every Mare.

35 Registered Dales Pony Mares have assisted nominations to Linnel Comet at 10/- each. Early Application for these, should be made to **Mr. Wm. Patterson, 5, Cattle Market, Hexham**, or to the Owner. Additional Registered Dales Mares at £1, and £1 for Foals.

All other Mares £1 at first service, and £1 10/- in March, 1920, unless mare is proved not to be in foal.

SEASON 1919.
Dales Pony Stallion

LINNEL COMET,

841,

Black. Foaled 1913. Height 14.1.

Holder of Board of Agriculture
Certificate of Soundness,

Premium for Dales Pony Improvement
Society's Western District, 1918.

—and for—

Hexham & East District, 1919.

Owner:

ROY B. CHARLTON,
Queens Letch,
Hexham-on-Tyne.

J. W. Hindson, Printer, 24, Dean St, Newcastle

1927

PREMIUM
Fell Pony Stallion

"LINNEL BOY"

1260.

Black Foaled 1923. 13·3 hands.

Sire: GUY MANNERING 937.
Dam: 3722 LINNEL FANCY.

Owner and Breeder
ROY B. CHARLTON,
Linnels,
Hexham-on-Tyne.

1934.

WAR OFFICE PREMIUM
FELL PONY STALLION

Linnel Gallant Boy

1704.

Black. Foaled 1930. 13-3½ h.h.
Sire: LINNEL MITE 1460 by
MOUNTAIN RANGER 598.
Dam: 5642 LINNEL FLUFF by
LINNEL MOOR BOY 1441.
G. Dam: 2916 LINNEL FLIRT by
DALESMAN 572.

The Property of—
ROY B. CHARLTON,
The Linnels, Hexham.
Groom—W. WILLIAMSON,
Bank End, Hesket New Market,
via Wigton.

Fell Pony Stallion

"HEATHER BOY AGAIN"

1446.

BROWN. FOALED 1924. 13·3 H.H.

Sire: Good Hope 1041 by Weardale Hero 607.
Dam: 4596 Heather May by Heather Boy 600 by Heather's Model.

This pony holds the £80 War Office Premium to travel APPLEBY DISTRICT Season 1929.

Groom:
JAMES WILSON,
BLACK BULL HOTEL,
APPLEBY.

Owner:
ROY B. CHARLTON,
THE LINNELS,
HEXHAM-ON-TYNE.

1927

The Dales Pony
Improvement Society
Premium Stallion

"LINNEL MIDNIGHT"

1261

Owner and Breeder
ROY B. CHARLTON, Jun.,
Linnels, Hexham.

"LINNEL COMET," DALES PONY STALLION
Winner of First Prize, Royal Show, Darlington
Championship Cup, London Pony Show, and War Office Premiums

plate 63

Extract from
'A Lifetime with Ponies'
by R. B. Charlton 1944

'I often think of the days when 'Linnel Comet' used to leave home on a Monday morning, to travel with a War Office Premium. He did a big journey every week throughout the summer season. He was timed to get back home at 7 o'clock on Friday evenings. I could set my clocks by him. I went out of my back door every Friday evening at 6.55 and stood and listened. There they were, the merry young man whistling for all he was worth, in step with one of the best Dales pony stallions that ever lived. Their speed was nearly five miles an hour, and they had walked 70 miles that week. They were both coming home, and they were very happy.'

Stallion Cards from the Linnel Stud

Images of working galloway pack ponies used in the carriage of lead ore during the 18th & early 19th centuries. An enthusiastic border collie is taking charge of a donkey. Once the lead ore was smelted the 'pigs' were transported by pack saddle or on carts.

plates 64-67

Right -
The galloways transport wood on their return journeys to the lead mines once the lead ore 'pigs' had been delivered.

Below -
A pack pony 'train'. The leading galloway pony, known as 'a raker' wearing a collar with bells, one in the centre and three on each side, was followed by the other pack ponies each carrying a load of 2 cwts.
Carrier ponies were not allowed to graze when on route as the grass would have been contaminated with lead.

Galloways carrying Wood.

plate 68

W GILBERT FOSTER.

plate 69

plate 70

Mr John Johnson & grandson John Pickworth, 1930s

Robert, Roy B. Charlton, Astrid, Vera Clare & Mary Clare in a tub trap pulled by Dolly, a Fell pony; Kathleen Scott standing to the right.

Examples of Suffolk Punch, Shire and Clydesdale stallions

"The horses are, for the most part, of the Clydesdale breed, though Shires and half-breds are also used for tillage work. Some farmers also breed a few hunters, or carriage horses, but the majority of them appear to prefer the heavier classes, where rearing and management involve less risk. Horses are kept to a very small extent on a pastoral farm, a single horse to take the farmer to market, to cart coals, wool and hay, frequently sufficing."

written in the late 19th century

The Next Generation of Horse Power

Abiove -
Miss Elizabeth Johnston c.1920

Above right -
Charbanc outing

Right -
R. W. Herdman
Haulage Contractor
Raw Green
Hexhamshire

plate 71

Harvest in the 'Shire

Threshing at Dukesfield Hall 1920s

Right - First left, Mr Blackburn; to his left, Syd White; man in centre of right, arms folded, Archie Scott; blonde child at front, George Crowe; far right, standing, Tommy Crowe.

The Kennedy family at work at
Embley in the 1950s.

Right -
Sydney White baling hay at Low Juniper
Farm c.1960

Below -
Back row - Trevor Simpson, Bob Bell, Syd
White, Alan Swallow. Front row - Gordon
Crowe, Ned Appleby, Eddie Dinning, Derek
White, Jackie Lowry, John Graham.

Below right -
Jonathan and Thomas Lee at Hackford 1948.

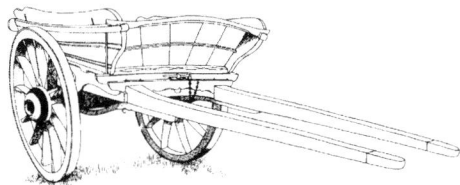

Hexhamshire coup cart

May Kennedy standing on hay cart, 1940s

Shire Families

The Bell Family 1910

Back row - Edwin, Margaret, Rebecca; front row - Edith, William & Annie Bell, William; front row - Robert & Sarah. Edith Bell (girl on far left) of Low Rawgreen was born in 1900. She married William Surtees in 1920. They emigrated to Harrami, Australia in 1926.

The Johnsons

Left -
John Johnson with daughters Dorothy and Elizabeth.

Below left -
'Granny Johnson' with a young John Pickworth
outside Dotland Park farmhouse c.1932.

The Olivers

Below -
William and Hannah Oliver of High Eshells c.1910

The family in the garden at Harwoodshield,
the road to Riddlehamhope in the distance. 1900

The Little Family

plates 72-75

Above -
Harwoodshield c.1900
Lady on left, Rebecca Little;
son Robert with pony;
daughters Bessie & Janet;
Mr George Little on right.

Left -
The Little family at
Harwoodshield.

Right -
The family at Blackhall in
their Studebaker car 1910.

The Lowdon Family

Above - Michael Hudson Makepeace, John William Lowdon and Robert Lowdon. c.1900

Right - Elizabeth (nee Makepeace) and Robert Lowdon on bridge near Riddlehamhope c.1915

Below - Pte. J. W. Lowdon, WWI

plates 76-78

The White Family

Above left -
Back row: John, Arthur, Dora, Alf, Fred.
Middle row: Lily, Jane & William, Flossie.
Front row: George and Clarence c.1900.

Above -
Lily and Dora White at Low Staples.

Left -
The wedding of Tom Wheatley and Dora White.

Left -
William & Matthew Henry White c.1870

Below -
At the Dukesfield Arches.
Arthur White on the left, lady in centre, Flossie, William White on the right.

plates 79-83

plates 84-87

Above -
Sydney White with his mother Evelyn c.1920

Above right -
Evelyn on the left and George White on the right:
Sydney's parents c.1900.

Thomas & Anne Simpson
of Low Juniper Farm

Ridley & Elsie White c.1900
Sydney's brother and sister

Acknowledgements

I would like to thank everyone who has kindly given permission for me to reproduce photographs and information. I apologise if I have missed names from the following list:

Alexander, Rosie: plates 45 & 46

Beamish Museum: plate 20 (90462), 22 (90463), 69 (15802), 71 (77051), page 137, top right (80241)

Blue Sky International Ltd: page 117 (391211/549978)

Bowman, Bob: page 80

Bramwell, Elizabeth: pages 71 - 73

Campbell, Maureen: plate 39 & page 87 (top left)

Carter, Ann: plates 47 & 48

Charlton, Ralph: plates 51 & 52; page 98 (top right)

Charlton, R B: 50, 54, 55; pages 133 & 136 (top right)

Craig, Margaret: page 142

Durham Records Office: plates 61(D/Wa3/6/19), 62 (D/Wa3/6/20) & 102 (1667-0007-0057)

Forster, Susan: figs 1 & 2 & plate 21

Gailiunas, Paul: plates 8 & 9

Gibson, Tony: page 108 (left)

Graham, Nancy: pages 121 (top left), 124 & 145 (lower left)

Hall, Jean: page 5

Kennedy, May: pages 81, 139, 141 & plate 27

Leybourne, Marjorie: line drawings on pages 11 & 23 & plates 56 & 57

Little, Mrs Adam: plates 1, 43, 44 & page 144

Makepeace, Jeff: plate 76

Martin, Betty: pages 146 & 147

Mike Anton Associates: plate 60

McKenzie, Cynthia: page 18

Northumberland Archives: Reproduced with permission of Northumberland Archives:
fig. 3 (OS map 2nd edition 1898); plate 19 (NRO 163/16 &17)), 34 (NRO 01876/D/876), 49 (NRO 1876-F-3472), page 132 (NRO 02168/5/10), (QSB 10, 12 & 106)

Pickworth, Pat: page 143

Science Museum/Science & Society Picture Library: plates 64 – 68

Short, Davy: top right page 121

Simpson, Marie: page 4, 138, 140 (top right & lower left), 148 & back cover painting

Sobell, Stefan: plates 2, 3, 5 &13

Steel, the family of the late Thomas Steel: plates 58 & 78

Tatman, Tim: page 36

Watson, Annie: pages 66 - 69

Weir, Albert: plate 35

Whatmough, Gill: pages 84, 130 & 131,

Grateful thanks to Rosemary Lee for allowing access to Riddlehamhope which is on private land: Pages 122 & 123: photographs of the interior & exterior of Riddlehamhope: Francesca Leslie & Niels Kristensen.
Thank you to Francesca for proof reading.

Front cover painting, property of the White family of Steel Hall.

Back cover painting, property of Marie Simpson.

End notes:

1. Ritchell's Account of Certain Charities, published 1780

2. A History of Northumberland, Volume IV, Part II, page 26

3. A Pack of Idle Sparks, edited by Greg Finch, page 135

4. A History of Northumberland, Volume IV, Part II

5. History of Hexham , A B Wright 1823, page 56

7. Dukesfield Document Project; Transcription by J. Gordon, 16-3-12, (NRO 672/E/1/E/3)

6. Northumberland Archives (NRO 00672/A/34/120); 8. (SANT/GEN/ECC/3/3/14); 9. (SANT/GEN/ECC/3/3/18); 11. (NRO QSB 18); 12. (NRO QSB 36); 13. (NRO QSB 106); 14. (NRO QSB 38); 15. (NRO QSB 1723)

Index

Auctions	90, 118 – 119,129 – 131	Newbiggin	54, 73, 79, 106 –111
Bastle, High Holmes	97	Poverty & paupers	30, 33, 37 - 40
Blackhall	90 – 94	Quarter Sessions	30 – 32
Box pews	14	Red Lead Mill	86
Bridge, Linnels	73, 103,105	Rev. Abraham Brown	7, 8, 16, 17, 18, 25, 26
Burials & funerals	24 – 29, 33	Rev. William Sisson	17, 23, 40, 43, 48, 65
Carrier ponies	134 – 135	Riddlehamhope	25,112 – 124, 145
Charity	30, 33, 39, 40, 41	Rowley Head	78, 89
Church gallery & music	8, 20, 21, 22	Schools	16, 42 - 57, 65, 88
Churchyard	24 - 29	Shire families	142
Corn mill, Linnels	98, 102, 103	Songs, Stories & Poems	70 – 78
Curates	7, 8, 16, 17, 18, 23, 25	Stained glass windows	7, 9, 13, 29
Devil's Water	63, 70, 71, 72, 73, 75, 76, 105	Stallions	132, 133, 136
Dipton Mill Inn	71, 73	Stotsfold farm	126, 127, 129, 130
Dukesfield smelt mill	58, 72,147,	Stotsfold Hall	125 – 131, 82, 85
Dye House	63,75, 87	St. Helen's Church	6 – 29
Farming	78, 138 – 141	Vicarage	19
Galloway ponies	134 – 135	War & soldiers	79 – 81
Halliwell Picnic	58 – 69	Westburnhope	84, 87, 88, 113
Halliwell Spa	58 – 64, 72, 84	Whitehall chapel	89
Harvest	138 -140	Whitley Chapel hall	83
Harwoodshield	87, 144	Whitley Chapel school	42 – 49, 65, 84, 88
Headstones	25 - 27	Workhouse	34 – 38
High Holmes	95 – 97		
Horse Power	132 – 135		
Juniper House	19		
Lilswood Chapel	86		
Lilswood School	50 – 53, 65, 88		
Linnels Corn Mill	99, 102, 103		
Linnel Stud	132 – 133		
Linnels, the	98 – 105		
Litharge farm	78, 86, 89		
Low Staples	146, 147		
Memories	82 – 89		
Mire Meadows	83, 84, 87		
Mollersteads	16, 18, 19		
Motor vehicles	137		

Bibliography

A History of Northumberland, Volume IV: Part II,
The Northumberland County History Committee 1897

A Pack of Idle Sparks, edited by Greg Finch;
Hexham Local History Society 2013

A Lifetime with Ponies, Roy B. Charlton;
Country Books 2003

Hexham Remembered, H. Kristensen & C. Dallison;
Wagtail Press 2006

Memories of Hexhamshire, H. Kristensen;
Wagtail Press 1999

The Life & Times of Thomas Dixon 1805 – 1871,
Dr S. M. Linsley; Wagtail Press 2006

Whitley St. Helen's Churchyard, H. Kristensen;
Wagtail Press 2003

Other Books Published by Wagtail Press:

A Coastal Voyage in Watercolour, Ron Thornton
Hexham Remembered, H. Kristensen & C. Dallison
Homecoming, poems by Wilfrid Gibson
Memories of Hexhamshire, H. Kristensen
Northumberland's Lost Houses, Jim Davidson
On the Trail of Red Squirrels, Will Nicholls
Sparty Lea; An Upland Leadmining Community,
   Jennifer W Norderhaug
The Diaries of William Brewis of Mitford 1833 – 1850,
   J. Foster & Dr M. Smith
The Life & Times of Thomas Dixon 1805 – 71,
   Dr S. M. Linsley
Thomas Irving's Journal 1851 – 1917,
   Edited by H. Kristensen
Whitley St. Helen's Churchyard, H. Kristensen

Wagtail Press
www.wagtailpress.co.uk